Dan Sareen

Theatre includes: *Shadows* (Tristan Bates Theatre, Edinburgh Festival Fringe & International Youth Arts Festival); *Other People's Teeth* (King's Head Theatre, Old Red Lion Theatre, Brighton Fringe & Edinburgh Festival Fringe); *Occam's Chainsaw* (Edinburgh Festival Fringe); *Soundtrack* (Little Leeds Fringe).

First published in the UK in 2023 by Aurora Metro Publications Ltd.

80 Hill Rise, Richmond TW10 6UB

www.aurorametro.com   info@aurorametro.com

FB/AuroraMetroBooks X @aurorametro

Instagram aurora_metro

Passing copyright © 2023 Dan Sareen

Cover image © 2023 Matt Martin, Shooting Theatre and Laura Whitehouse, Mighty Fine Design

All rights are strictly reserved.

For rights enquiries including performing rights, please contact the publisher: rights@aurorametro.com

No part of this publication may be reproduced, stored in or introduced into a retrieval system, or transmitted in any form, or by any means (electronic, mechanical, photocopying, recording or otherwise) without the prior permission of the publisher. Any person who does any unauthorised act in relation to this publication may be liable to criminal prosecution and civil claims for damages.

This paperback is sold subject to the condition that it shall not, by way of trade or otherwise, be lent, resold, hired out, or otherwise circulated without the publisher's prior consent in any form of binding or cover other than that in which it is published and without a similar condition being imposed on the subsequent purchaser.

Printed in the UK by 4edge printers on sustainably resourced paper

ISBNs:

978-1-910798-64-5 (print)

978-1-910798-65-2 (ebook)

Passing

by
Dan Sareen

AURORA METRO BOOKS

Thanks

For this production:

Helen and Shiv Sareen; Zoë Edwards; Arts Council England; Unity Theatre Trust; Daniel Cooper; Prem Sareen

For development:

Phillipa Flynn; Hannah Khalique-Brown, Adam Karim and Ranjit Krishnamma; Nic Connaughton and the Pleasance Theatre; Neil D'Souza; Gavi Singh Chera, Komal Amin and Iwan Davies; Karim Shabankareh

For encouragement and advice:

Azan Ahmed; Jess Williams; Ross White; Solvene Tiffou; Debbie Korley; Iain McManus; Chris Foxon; Ebenezer Bamgboye; Tom Reed; Chris Thorpe; Layla Madanat; Phoebe Hyder

CONTENTS

About the Company 6
Cast and Creative Team 10
Biographies 11
Playtext: *Passing* 15

PARK THEATRE

Park Theatre was founded by Artistic Director, Jez Bond and Creative Director Emeritus, Melli Marie. The building opened in May 2013 and, with 12 West End transfers, two National Theatre transfers and 14 national tours in ten years, quickly garnered a reputation as a key player in the London theatrical scene. Park Theatre has received six Olivier nominations, won numerous Off West End Offie Awards, and won The Stage's Fringe Theatre of the Year and Accessible Theatre Award.

Park Theatre is an inviting and accessible venue, delivering work of exceptional calibre in the heart of Finsbury Park. We work with writers, directors and designers of the highest quality to present compelling, exciting and beautifully told stories across our two intimate spaces.

Our programme encompasses a broad range of work from classics to revivals with a healthy dose of new writing, producing in-house as well as working in partnership with emerging and established producers. We strive to play our part within the UK's theatre ecology by offering mentoring, support and opportunities to artists and producers within a professional theatre-making environment.

Our Creative Learning strategy seeks to widen the number and range of people who participate in theatre, and provides opportunities for those with little or no prior contact with the arts.

In everything we do we aim to be warm and inclusive; a safe, welcoming and wonderful space in which to work, create and visit.

***** "A five-star neighbourhood theatre"
— Independent

As a registered charity [number 1137223] with no public subsidy, we rely on the kind support of our donors and volunteers. To find out how you can get involved visit parktheatre.co.uk

For Park Theatre:

Artistic Director

Jez Bond

Executive Director

Catherine McKinney

Community Engagement Manager – Carys Rose Thomas

Creative Learning Leaders – Amy Allen, Toby Hampton, Kieran Rose, Vanessa Sampson

Development Director – Tania Dunn

Development & Producing Coordinator – Ellen Harris

Finance Director – Elaine Lavelle

Finance Officer – Nicola Brown

General Manager – Tom Bailey

Deputy General Manager – David Hunter

Producer Programmer – Amelia Cherry

Administrator – Mariah Sayer

ABOUT THE COMPANY

Access Coordinator – David Deacon

Duty Venue Managers – Daisy Bates, Leiran Gibson, **Gareth Hackney,** Zara Naeem, Laura Riseborough, Natasha Green, David Hunter, Shaun Joynson, Leena Makoff, Wayne Morris, Nick Raistrick

Supervisors Park Pizza – Daisy Bates, Luke Brock

Bar Team – George Gehm, John Burman, Bradly Doko, Hugo Harrison, Alex Kristoffy, Vanessa Restivo, Bonnie Shapland-Hill, Julia Skinner, Maddie Stoneman, Maria Ziolkowska

Sales & Marketing Director – Dawn James

Head of Ticketing – Matthew Barker

Senior Marketing Officer – Anna Charlesworth

Senior Box Office Supervisor – Natasha Green
Box Office Supervisors – Jacquie Cassidy, Gareth Hackney, Kyanne Smith, Maddie Stoneman

Public Relations – Mobius Industries

Technical and Buildings Manager – Gianluca Zona

Deputy Technical and Buildings Manager – Teddy Nash

Venue Technician – Michael Bird

Supported by Unity Theatre Trust

WANT THE MOON

Founded in 2018 by graduates of the University of Leeds, Dan Sareen, Ellen Harris and Jessica Williams, Want the Moon Theatre Company was set up to produce new writing tackling modern, relevant and diverse themes. The company's first show, *Other People's Teeth* (★★★★, The Scotsman), was performed at Brighton Fringe, multiple fringe venues in London including the King's Head Theatre and the Old Red Lion Theatre, and Edinburgh Festival Fringe. Want the Moon followed this with *Shadows* (★★★★, Broadway Baby), which was performed at the Tristan Bates Theatre and Edinburgh Festival Fringe. This show was invited to be performed at the prestigious National Student Drama Festival in 2020.

Supported using public funding by
ARTS COUNCIL ENGLAND

LOTTERY FUNDED

ABOUT THE COMPANY

Cast and Creatives

CAST
RACHEL SINGH | AMY-LEIGH HICKMAN
YASH SINGH | BHASKER PATEL
RUTH SINGH | CATHERINE CUSACK
MATT | JACK FLAMMIGER
DAVID SINGH | KISHORE WALKER

CREATIVES
WRITER & PRODUCER | DAN SAREEN
DIRECTOR | IMY WYATT CORNER
COMPANY STAGE MANAGER AND ASSISTANT DIRECTOR | CASSIA THAKKAR
LIGHTING DESIGN | CATJA HAMILTON
PRODUCER | ELLEN HARRIS
MARKETING | CUP OF AMBITION
PR | CHLOE NELKIN CONSULTING
IMAGE DESIGN | LAURA WHITEHOUSE
PHOTOGRAPHY | MATT MARTIN
INITIAL ARTWORK | CHLOE BRIDGE
PHOTOSHOOT SET DRESSING | MAUD FLEMINGER THOMSON
IMAGE EDITING | TABBY THOMPSON

Biographies

CAST

Amy-Leigh Hickman (Rachel Singh)
Theatre includes: East is East (National Theatre); Beautiful Thing (Tobacco Factory); South Pacific; Fiddler on the Roof (UK Productions); Joseph and the Amazing Technicolour Dreamcoat; Half a Six Pence (Bill Kenwright).
Television includes: You; Ackley Bridge; Our Girl; Ruby Speaking; Tracy Beaker Returns; Strike Back; Safe; Innocent.
Film includes: The Left Behind

Bhasker Patel (Yash Singh)
Theatre includes: The Vote, Silence (Donmar Theatre); Anthony and Cleopatra (Liverpool Playhouse); A Map of the World; Tartuffe; The Magic Carpet; Wicked Yaar (Royal National Theatre); Aladdin and the Enchanted Lamp (Bristol Old Vic); Blood (Royal court/Joint Stock); Comedians (Lyrics – Belfast); Comedy of Errors (Octagon – Bolton); Mr. Robinsons Party (Tricycle Theatre); Playing With Fire; Royal Hunt of the Sun (National Theatre); The Great Celestial Cow (Royal Court); Timon of Athens (Young Vic); Vigilantes (Arts Theatre, West End); Whale (Sheffield Crucible); Zameen (Soho Theatre).
Film includes: Snowden; Anuvahood; Kidulthood; Partition; Transatlantic; Immaculate Conception; Flight; Arabian Nights; Mad Dogs; Thunderbirds; Bridget Jones: The Edge of Reason; The Family Portrait; Rent; Golden Eye.
TV includes: Emmerdale; Holby City; A & E; Birds of a Feather; Brookside; Casualty; Coronation Street; Dalziel and Pascoe; Fifteen Stories High; Holby Blue; Katy Brand's Big Ass Show; My Family; NCS; Only Fools and Horses; Skins; The Bill.

Catherine Cusack (Ruth Singh)
Theatre includes: Further than the Furthest Thing (Minack); Super High Resolution (Soho Theatre); Spring Awakening

(Almeida); The Shadow Factory (Nuffield, Southampton); Judith: A Parting from the Body, Fragile, Factory Girls (Arcola); Dancing at Lughnasa, The Crucible (Lyric, Belfast); The Seagull (Headlong Tour); All That Fall (Jermyn Street Theatre/New York); Bingo (Chichester Festival Theatre/Young Vic); The Two Character Play (Jermyn Street Theatre/Provincetown, USA); The Early Bird, The Gigli Concert (Finborough); What Fatima Did (Hampstead); Mary Stuart (National Theatre of Scotland); Our Lady of Sligo (NT/Out of Joint); Prayers of Sherkin (Old Vic); Mrs Warren's Profession (Lyric Hammersmith); Phaedra's Love (Gate); The Glass Menagerie (Bolton).
Television includes: Doctors; Endeavour; Hollyoaks; The Last Days of Anne Boleyn; Jonathan Creek; Ballykissangel; The Bill; Cadfael; Coronation Street; Dr. Who.
Film includes: Finding Neverland; Conspiracy of Silence; Boxed; The Lonely Passion of Judith Hearne.
Radio: Catherine is a regular on BBC Radio.

Jack Flammiger (Matt)
Jack trained at the Royal Academy of Dramatic Art (RADA)
Theatre includes: COPS (Southwark Playhouse); The Drought (King's Head Theatre & Old Red Lion Theatre); Jury Duty Live (Theatre Deli); The Inquest (Theatre Deli)
Radio includes: Ulverton: Wing/Here/Expedition (Radio 4)
Film includes: Just Men

Kishore Walker (David Singh)
Kishore trained at Guildhall School of Music & Drama.
Theatre includes: The Boys Are Kissing (Theatre503).
Television includes: Queenie; Doctors.

CREATIVES

Dan Sareen (Writer/Producer)
Theatre includes: Shadows (Tristan Bates Theatre, Edinburgh Festival Fringe & International Youth Arts Festival); Other People's Teeth (King's Head Theatre, Old Red Lion Theatre, Brighton Fringe & Edinburgh Festival Fringe); Occam's Chainsaw (Edinburgh Festival Fringe); Soundtrack (Little Leeds Fringe).

Imy Wyatt Corner (Director)
Imy trained at Bristol Old Vic Theatre School.
Direction includes: Duck (Arcola Theatre, Jermyn st Theatre), Happy Yet? (International Theatre, Frankfurt), Snail (Vault Festival), Walk Swiftly & With Purpose (Theatre503, North Wall Arts Centre), Baby, What Blessings (Bunker Theatre, Theatre503), BEASTS (Omnibus Theatre, Edinburgh Fringe), Felt (Southwark Playhouse), Gaslight (Playground Theatre), A Midsummer Nights Dream (The Grove DIY skatepark) and Humane (Pleasance Theatre).
Associate/ Assistant Direction includes: Private Lives (West End), Relatively Speaking (Theatre Royal Bath/ UK Tour), The Dance of Death (Theatre Royal Bath UK Tour), Love All (Jermyn st Theatre) & The Straw Chair (Finborough Theatre).
Imy was a Creative Associate at Jermyn St Theatre (2022/3) and is currently an Artistic Associate at Arcola Theatre.

Ellen Harris (Co-Producer)
Theatre includes: Shadows (Tristan Bates Theatre, Edinburgh Festival Fringe & International Youth Arts Festival); One Giant Leap (Edinburgh Festival Fringe); Other People's Teeth (King's Head Theatre, Old Red Lion Theatre, Brighton Fringe & Edinburgh Festival Fringe); Brothers (Edinburgh Festival Fringe); Occam's Chainsaw (Edinburgh Festival Fringe).

Ellen is currently the Development and Producing Coordinator at Park Theatre and has worked as an Assistant Producer on their in-house productions since May 2022.

Catja Hamilton (Lighting Designer)
Theatre credits include: The Importance of Being... Earnest? (UK tour); Sorry We Didn't Die At Sea (Park Theatre); Birthright (Finborough Theatre); Public: The Musical (Pleasance); Wonderdrug (Pleasance); Agrippina (Jackson's Lane); The Oyster Problem (Jermyn Street Theatre); Five Years With The White Man (King's Head Theatre); SNAIL (VAULT Festival); Acid's Reign (VAULT Festival); Lesbian Space Crime (Soho Theatre); Cassandra (Omnibus Theatre and UK tour); Time and Tide (UK tour); Another America (Park Theatre); Paradise Lost (The Shipwright); The Boatswain's Mate (Arcola and UK tour); An Intervention (Riverside Studios); Lizard King (UK tour); The 4th Country (Park Theatre); Patient Light (The Undercroft).

Cassia Thakker (Assistant Director/Stage Manager)
Cassia trained at Cambridge University.
Direction includes: Reparations (Riverside Studios, Omnibus Theatre); God Forgive Us, We Have Burnt a Saint (Riverside Studios); The Passion (White Bear Theatre, Corpus Playrooms); Queen Anne (ADC Theatre).
Associate/ Assistant Direction includes: Lotus Beauty (Hampstead Theatre); The Marlowe Showcase (Etcetera Theatre); Angels in America; Perestroika (ADC Theatre); Macbeth (ADC Theatre); Great Mother, Iya Ayaba (Corpus Playrooms); The Nature of a Curve (Corpus Playrooms).
Other theatrical work includes: the Cold War Free Festival (Almedia Young Producers Program); stage management for Lotus Beauty (Hampstead Theatre), West London Playwrights Group (Bush Theatre).

Passing

Dan Sareen

The play was first performed at Park Theatre, London on November 1st, 2023.

Directed by Imy Wyatt Corner.

Characters

RACHEL
DAVID
MATT
YASH
RUTH

ACT I, SCENE 1

Lights up. The reception room of a house. Two sofas sit downstage, a coffee table between them. The room also contains a record player and speakers – which at open are playing Ravi Shankar's "The Sounds of India". Alongside this is a stand or set of shelves containing a great many vinyl records, and plenty of other items and furniture making up a normal home. There are two entrances – one leads to a small foyer and the front door, the other to the hall and the rest of the house.

RACHEL is attempting to hang fairy lights across the back of the room. There should already be many sets of lights twisted around all of the objects in the room, and Rachel is hanging the last of them. She plugs in all the lights, and goes to turn them on, but hesitates. Instead, she approaches a silk sari which is draped over a sofa, holding it up against her body, trying to work out how to fold it. DAVID enters very quietly from the foyer. When he speaks, she jumps slightly.

DAVID So this is Diwali, is it?

RACHEL Bloody hell, David.

RACHEL drops the sari back over the sofa and hurries to turn off the record. She takes a moment to compose herself, then initiates a hug, a bit awkwardly.

RACHEL Diwale ki Shubhkamnayein.

DAVID If you say so.

RACHEL (*Indicating the lights*) What do you think?

DAVID Seems like a... fire hazard. What's it all for?

RACHEL The big finale of course.

DAVID We're going to... electrocute ourselves?

RACHEL We'll turn on the lights.
DAVID Ah, just like at Christmas.
RACHEL No. Nothing like that. It's the festival of lights.
DAVID Has Mum seen it?
RACHEL She is aware I'm decorating...
DAVID And what does *he* have to say?
RACHEL Dad? Quite little. Do you think it looks ok?
DAVID No idea. What's it supposed to look like?
RACHEL (*Holding up sari*) What about this... Do you think it's alright? Does it look...
DAVID Yeah it's... I'm not really sure what you want me to say, Rach.
RACHEL Maybe that you're happy to be here and that we're finally doing this, finally investing in our heritage-
DAVID I mean honestly...

She looks at him sharply.

RACHEL What?
DAVID I dunno.
RACHEL No, go on.
DAVID Well... It's all a bit much, isn't it? Just feels... Strange. For us to be... For our family to be –
RACHEL It's not strange. How can you say that?
DAVID Alright, don't jump down my throat. It's just, we're hardly the most suitable candidates-
RACHEL Don't be so stupid. Why do you always-
DAVID You asked what I thought! I'm only saying, we're basically –
RACHEL Please. Don't, today.
DAVID Fine, fine. But you did ask. What? Why are

you looking at me like that?

RACHEL Look, thank you for coming and everything... I'm really glad that you did.

DAVID You're welcome.

RACHEL Today it's paramount that everything go... Just – Please... Don't *do* anything. Ok?

DAVID Don't do anything? Can I breathe?

RACHEL Don't screw anything up, ok? Please? Between you and –

DAVID Have you given him this warning speech?

RACHEL Please. It's too important.

DAVID Why's that?

She doesn't respond, busying herself. Slight pause. DAVID clearly has something to say.

DAVID Is Grandad going to make an appearance?

RACHEL Dad's going to pick him up later. We didn't think he could handle the whole day.

DAVID Really? He isn't –

RACHEL If he comes any earlier he just has a nap anyway.

DAVID Right. Probably... Best, yeah. Have you...

RACHEL What?

DAVID Seen him recently?

RACHEL Have you?

DAVID I call him a lot.

RACHEL I'm sure you do.

DAVID Just can't always... Getting away from the flat, even at weekends. Seriously though...

RACHEL Seriously?

DAVID Yeah, let's try seriousness. Just this once. Is he –

The sound of the front door can be heard opening.

YASH (*From off*) If you ask them, in the café or wherever...

RACHEL   Too late.

YASH   Are you going to take your shoes off? To grind the beans for you, even if you ask for a cafetiere grind –

YASH enters from the foyer, speaking to but not looking at MATT. MATT carries a box or two with bottles of beer. YASH sees DAVID.

YASH   David...

DAVID   Father.

RACHEL   Get everything you wanted?

MATT   Just some essentials!

He goes to kiss RACHEL, and she somewhat reluctantly offers her cheek.

DAVID   Matthew, lovely to see you again. Thought this was strictly a Singh family event.

DAVID goes to shake MATT's hand, and he struggles to do so whilst still holding the box.

MATT   Always happy for an excuse to celebrate.

DAVID   I'm sure you had a choice in the matter.

YASH (*To DAVID*) No weekend plans, then?

RACHEL (*To MATT*) You can put that down.

MATT   You ok?

RACHEL   Fine.

MATT has put the crate down.

YASH   You couldn't put that in the kitchen, could you?

RACHEL   Dad, he's not –

MATT   Don't worry, I've got it!

MATT picks up the crate.

DAVID Oh, but please finish your conversation. Sounded fascinating.

YASH I was saying...

MATT has gone towards the hall, but now lingers awkwardly holding the crate, waiting for YASH to speak. Slight pause.

RACHEL Coffee, Dad. Something about coffee grinding.

YASH Even if you ask for a cafetiere grind, they will do it too finely. You need a coarse grind for cafetiere.

MATT That's really interesting–

YASH I let Matt make the coffee this morning.

DAVID Oh no.

RACHEL It wasn't that bad.

MATT You said you liked it.

YASH Love makes people say crazy things.

This has left an awkward tension, though YASH takes no notice.

RACHEL He just needs another chance.

YASH It is time for second cup.

MATT A second cup? It's only–

DAVID Clearly you're not abreast of the rigorous routine.

RACHEL You can go put that down.

MATT It's ok.

RACHEL Maybe you could supervise this time, Dad?

MATT I'm sure I can get it. I just need to –

YASH Grind the beans more coarsely.

DAVID Make sure the water temperature is between 92 and 96 degrees.

RACHEL Fill it halfway and let it bloom for 30 to 40 seconds. Then fill the rest –

YASH And let it sit for exactly 3 minutes and 20 seconds before plunging.

MATT Exactly, I'll just... do all of that.

RACHEL Off you go.

She squeezes his arm lightly before he exits to the hall.

DAVID Think you bought enough?

YASH Always a pleasure to have you visit.

Slight pause. In the silence, RACHEL gives both of them warning looks. She looks like she will try to say something, but is saved from doing so by the sound of the front door opening.

RUTH (*from off*) Only me!

RACHEL Perfect timing.

RUTH enters from the foyer. She carries multiple shopping bags. MATT enters quickly from the hall.

RUTH Hello, hello.

MATT Hi! Do you need a hand with those?

RUTH Oh, thank you. Just pop them in the kitchen.

YASH What's happened to the coffee?

DAVID Morning, mum.

RUTH Oh, hello darling!

RUTH hugs DAVID tightly.

RACHEL Did you find everything? Thank you for going for me.

RUTH What are mum's for. I can see you've been working hard since I left.

RACHEL Do you like it?

RUTH Yes... Yes, of course.

RACHEL It'll look better later when it's all lit up, and dark outside.

RUTH Yes.

RACHEL What?

RUTH Nothing. It's wonderful, really.

DAVID She's worried about how you're going to get it all back in the box.

YASH Without tangling it all up.

RUTH Don't be silly.

RACHEL I'm not just going to leave you to do it, mum.

DAVID Like how you left her to do the shopping, you mean?

RUTH Shush now, let's not make a scene in front of company.

DAVID He's not even in the room...

RACHEL has been looking at a scrap of paper with writing all over it.

RACHEL OK. Now focus on me for a second please, now you're all here. No time to waste. Have a seat.

YASH Family meeting, is it? Shouldn't we get Matt in here?

RACHEL In a second –

RUTH Is everything alright with you two, Rach? I noticed this morning –

RACHEL Not the time, Mum.

YASH Nothing's wrong, Ruth. If anything...

Slight pause.

RACHEL What?

YASH What? Nothing.

RACHEL "If anything" what?

YASH Just... I would say that absolutely nothing is

wrong. The opposite is true. I heard...

DAVID   Did a little birdie tell you?

YASH   What? Yes.

RUTH   Don't interrupt his train of thought.

YASH   I heard that maybe... Potentially...

DAVID   Less a train of thought, more a hearse of thought...

YASH   Things might be looking quite... Serious. Between you two.

RUTH   Let's not get carried away.

DAVID   Exactly how serious are we talking?

RACHEL   Can we stop this now?

YASH   I would guess –

RUTH   Oh, don't guess.

YASH   An educated guess. I think a little bird might be about to...

He makes a gesture of fluttering wings with his arms.

RUTH   How are we supposed to interpret that?

DAVID   Question. Is this the same little birdie that told you the exciting news, or a different little bird?

YASH   What are you talking about?

RUTH   What are *you* talking about?

YASH   I think I was very clear.

DAVID   Trust me, you weren't.

RACHEL   Flying the nest. The little bird is leaving the nest.

YASH   Exactly. Somebody understands me.

DAVID   Is the little bird leaving the nest?

Pause. They all look at RACHEL.

RACHEL   No. I mean... Not never, just... I'm aware

I'm in my mid twenties living at home so I'm not going to say it's not a possibility, I guess. But not right this second, no. There are no imminent plans –

YASH Well, no smoke without fire, as they say.

RUTH Perhaps we should put a pin in this one for now...

RACHEL Let's put a pin in all of it because I have something to say –

DAVID And it's not about little birds?

RACHEL It's not about birds, or relationships, or smoke and fire, and if the three of you don't be quiet and start listening to me then smoke and fire is what you will find yourselves engulfed in.

Slight pause.

DAVID What a weird threat.

YASH What does it mean, you're going to set us on fire?

RUTH I think it was more metaphorical.

DAVID Like your anger will be... Ablaze?

RACHEL Literal smoke and fire.

YASH She is going to set us alight.

DAVID I don't think she would. Wouldn't follow through.

RUTH But what a spectacle that would make for the festival of lights...

RACHEL glares at them.

RUTH And now we're putting a pin in everything. Hush, hush, everyone.

Pause while RACHEL composes herself to speak.

RACHEL I just wanted to say, quickly before Matt's done with the coffee... Look, I know this is maybe all a bit much, and I wanted to say... Thank you. Thanks for being here, for putting up with everything... Thank you, family, for being here for our big inaugural celebration of Diwali. So, there it is. That's all.

Silence, they don't know what to say.

RACHEL   What?

RUTH   Oh, that was it?

RACHEL   Yeah, what? I'm not allowed to say thank you?

YASH   It's a little out of character...

DAVID   Not sure how you got from threatening to set us on fire to thanking us, quite so quickly.

RACHEL   This time, the festival, it's all about new beginnings and prosperity, and being grateful and kind to loved ones...

YASH   Ah right. This is just a Diwali thing.

DAVID   I was worried for a second that she'd hit her head or something.

RACHEL   Maybe this is why I never... Look I just want to make today really special, so that it doesn't feel... I don't know. Not normal, for us.

Slight pause. The family are slightly taken aback by RACHEL's demeanour. RUTH comforts her.

RUTH   We are all very glad to hear your words of thanks, Rachel. Aren't we? And we're all more than happy to help out and make the celebration special.

DAVID   So happy.

RACHEL   Good.

Pause.

YASH   It's definitely been more than 3 minutes 20.

DAVID   He's over-extracted. Textbook error.

MATT bursts in at this point with a tray laden with mugs.

MATT   Sorry didn't mean to interrupt a family meeting! Here we are.

YASH   Are we having tea?

MATT   What? I thought you wanted –

RACHEL   Those are the mugs he uses for tea.

DAVID   It's a steep learning curve.

YASH drinks.

YASH   Some improvement.

MATT   Is it ok?

RACHEL   It's much better. Well done.

RUTH   Yes, lovely, lovely.

MATT (*to RACHEL*) Are you ok?

RACHEL   Yeah. I'm fine. Are you?

MATT   Yeah, of course. I'm fine. Just making sure…

RUTH   Well. So nice to have everyone here. Can't remember the last time we had everyone together. With Matt too.

DAVID   Not everyone's here.

RUTH   Grandad's coming later.

YASH   There's too much going on for him.

DAVID   He can't sit here and enjoy the atmosphere? I'm sure he'd like –

YASH   How would you know what he'd like?

RUTH   Alright, hush now. The carer's with him this morning, and he'll be fresh for when we collect him later.

MATT   Makes perfect sense to me.

RUTH   You'll get used to this Matt. Now, Rachel, let me run through this checklist with you, make sure we've got everything. Talk amongst yourselves.

DAVID   No thank you.

RUTH   I purchased the mithai...

She pronounces it "mih-thay".

RACHEL   It's mithai, mum. The t is hard. "mih-tie".

RUTH   Mithai, yes. Well, I won't run through all the individual sweets then, I'll just get all the names wrong!

RACHEL   As long as you got the Gulab Jamun, that's my favourite.

MATT   Which one is that?

RUTH   The little balls in the sugar syrup?

YASH   Acquired taste.

MATT   Oh, do you think?

DAVID   Am I the only one who hasn't tried this goo –lab – What is it?

RUTH   You can try it later.

YASH   You have to be in a certain frame of mind...

RACHEL   This is more a conversation for just the two of us.

YASH   They're very sweet, it's impossible to eat more than one.

RACHEL   You can watch me eat more than one later.

MATT   I know what you mean.

RACHEL   You like them.

MATT   I know I do, just... I know what he means... About the sweetness...

DAVID   This is quite the build up. What time is mithai time?

He pronounces it "my-tie".

RACHEL   I will hit you.

RUTH   I don't know if there is a specific time.

YASH Wait until my dad's here, I think.

RUTH He won't eat any.

YASH He has to eat something. He might like them.

RUTH You know what the doctor said about sugar…

DAVID What did they say?

YASH He's fine.

RACHEL Let's not do this now.

DAVID What does that mean, he's "fine", if he can't have sugar –

YASH He can eat what he wants to eat. He has that right.

RUTH Alright. The checklist, the checklist.

RACHEL Chiwda?

RUTH Um…

RACHEL Bombay mix, mum.

RUTH Ah yes, check.

YASH There goes my diet.

RACHEL Stuff for the tea?

RUTH Assam, cloves, cinnamon sticks, ginger, cardamom pods. Check, check, check, check, check. We've already got milk. I couldn't get black peppercorns so you'll have to make do with green.

DAVID All that goes in the tea?

YASH It's an –

RACHEL If you say acquired taste, I swear…

MATT Ooh, not sure I'll…

RACHEL You'll try it.

MATT Apparently I'll try it.

DAVID Can't be any worse than –

RACHEL Chutney ingredients?

MATT Were you going to say the coffee I made?

DAVID 'course not.

RUTH Yes. Dates, tamarind paste, fresh mint, lots of yoghurt, chillies – everything!

RACHEL Thank you.

RUTH And I stopped by Karen's to get my blender back. So we don't have to use the pestle and mortar for all of it.

YASH I hope you got my barbecue tongs too.

RUTH Another job for another day, dear.

DAVID You never barbecue anything.

YASH Not without my tongs...

RUTH You weren't very specific about the appetizers, so I just got a selection. Bhaji's and samosas and things. They just go in the oven.

RACHEL They won't be very authentic.

RUTH What else can we do? We can't make them from scratch.

RACHEL Next year maybe.

DAVID This is a yearly thing?

MATT It's actually like the Hindi version of Christmas.

RACHEL Nothing like Christmas.

MATT No, I just meant... they celebrate it every year.

DAVID I meant yearly for our family. Not just a one off thing?

RUTH So that should be everything –

RACHEL Did you get some matches?

Pause.

RUTH I–
RACHEL You didn't get any matches?
RUTH I thought I had everything on the list.
DAVID What do we need matches for?
RACHEL How can you possibly have failed to notice the multitudes of candles around you?
MATT Diyas, they're called –
DAVID Oh yeah.
YASH You'll just have to use the thing.
RACHEL What thing?
DAVID What are they for?
MATT You light them –
YASH The thing in the kitchen.
DAVID Yes, obviously you light them.
RUTH What on earth are you talking about?
DAVID What do you light them for?
RACHEL How can this have happened?
YASH The thing that – lights...
MATT It's a ritual.
RUTH The fire lighter?
YASH Yes, exactly.
MATT It's the festival of lights, so –
RUTH We can't use that.
YASH Why not?
DAVID So what?
MATT So, they light the candles... as part of the –
RUTH It's run out of lighter fluid.
RACHEL Don't you have a lighter?
DAVID Why would I randomly have a lighter to hand?

MATT What about putting the hobs on and lighting the candles from that?

RUTH They're electric hobs, dear, not gas.

YASH And we can't use –

RACHEL No. We can't. We can't use matches that we don't have or a gas hob that's actually electric, or a fire lighter that in itself cannot perform the single function it was built for – to light fires.

RUTH Ok, let's calm down –

RACHEL Don't tell me to –

YASH Don't shout.

RACHEL This isn't shouting. This is a forceful tone. I can't believe you've forgotten the one thing –

RUTH I thought I had everything on the list.

RACHEL Everything? You missed the most essential… I can't even –

DAVID Hardly the most essential –

RACHEL Tell us again, Matt, just exactly what this festival is?

MATT The festival of –

RACHEL The festival of lights.

YASH Don't shout at your mother.

RACHEL I'm not shouting.

DAVID It really kind of sounds like –

RACHEL I promise you. This is not shouting.

MATT It's really not.

DAVID What's the big deal?

MATT It's all part of it…

DAVID So we don't light the candles, there's still all the fairy lights.

RACHEL We have to light the lamps. We have to light

the lamps and put them outside the door and let them burn after the sun goes down to ward off Yama.

DAVID It's like you're speaking a different language.

YASH *(Getting up)* This is silly. I can just pop down the road to get –

RACHEL Sit down. We're already running behind, don't have time to...

MATT Rach, don't panic...

RUTH I'm sorry –

RACHEL You're sorry?

RUTH I really thought –

RACHEL I knew this was going to happen. Why can't it just work, why can't it be easy?

MATT Nothing's gone wrong, Rach, nothing we can't fix.

RACHEL It's not right, it's got to be right!

YASH For the last time –

RACHEL Oh, for god's sake.

YASH Do not shout –

RACHEL I AM NOT SHOUTING. THIS WOULD BE SHOUTING.

Pause.

YASH Well, exactly. Don't do that.

MATT Alright. It's ok. We've got a little problem. No need to get so worked up, is there? Come on.

RUTH I really am very sorry.

MATT None of that, you've done an amazing job with everything you got for today.

RACHEL But we need –

MATT And we'll get them. Someone is going to pick up your Grandad at some point, right?

YASH That's me.

MATT So I'm sure it wouldn't be too difficult or take too long to stop somewhere on the way, or on the way back, and pick up a box of matches, right?

YASH I think I can manage that.

MATT So, problem solved.

RACHEL We've wasted loads of time. We need to get dressed.

Nobody moves.

RACHEL Well go on then.

RUTH Yes, absolutely. Let's go get changed, Yash.

YASH What's wrong with what I'm wearing?

RUTH Oh, really. I left your clothes on your bed for you!

YASH I thought that was the ironing pile.

RUTH pulls YASH to the hall. RACHEL picks up her sari. She turns to DAVID, who has not moved.

DAVID What's going on? This is –

RACHEL Just play along, please. I'm asking nicely. There's a shirt on your bed.

DAVID Fine. Just... Lay off mum a bit, will you?

RACHEL I didn't –

DAVID I'm asking nicely too...

He exits, smirking. RACHEL and MATT clock each other and the fact that they are alone.

RACHEL Don't ask me if I'm ok.

MATT I won't.

He chooses his words carefully.

MATT Is... Everything alright?

RACHEL Is that supposed to be funny?

MATT   I just meant... Is everything back on track? With today?

RACHEL   Depends how long everyone takes to get changed. Will you help me with...

MATT   Of course. Do you know –

RACHEL   I think so, I watched a video...

They proceed to try and dress RACHEL in the sari.

MATT   I'm really sorry.

RACHEL   Hold this, I have to tuck it in first. And then spin...

MATT   About yesterday... I shouldn't have left things that way. Over the shoulder?

RACHEL   You have to make pleats.

MATT   What are pleats?

RACHEL   Like – little folds. Like this.

MATT   I didn't explain it properly. I was going to come last night and stay over like you said –

RACHEL   I was being a control freak. I'm being a control freak. I can't help it. You're pleating wrong. See what I mean?

MATT   You want everything to be perfect.

RACHEL   I just wanted you to be here so that you could shower and get ready here, and –

MATT   But like I said –

RACHEL   Let's not go through the whole thing again.

MATT   Right. You're right. Like this?

RACHEL   Yeah, that's... Fine, I think. You get why...

MATT   Yes, I do.

RACHEL   Washing yourself clean, it's one of the traditions. And lighting the diyas too. We've got to do everything...

MATT   But Rach, when you plan anything...

RACHEL   Things go wrong, I know. And I'm making a big deal out of everything, I don't mean to be angry... Things can go wrong... I just don't want them to go wrong because people aren't taking this seriously.

MATT   Everyone's –

RACHEL   Humouring me.

MATT   That's not true. We can all see how important this is to you. So everyone's happy to go along with it, because they love you.

RACHEL   Ok.

MATT   Ok?

RACHEL   Yeah. Ok. Didn't I just say ok?

MATT   Ok. But I am sorry. About the washing. I mean I have showered. And I want you to understand my point of view, do you get why I wanted to –

RACHEL   Matt. It's fine. You're here. That's what matters.

MATT   So why do I get the feeling that it's not fine?

RACHEL   What do you mean?

MATT   You feel so far away.

RACHEL   You're literally standing right next to me.

MATT   Not physically, I mean...

RACHEL   You couldn't be much closer. Now over the shoulder...

MATT   How long?

RACHEL   Down to the back of my knee... Thanks.

They have finished tying the sari by this point.

MATT   You look...

RACHEL   Yes?

MATT   Stunning. Dazzling. Beautiful. Take your pick.

RACHEL   Stop it.
MATT   Mesmerising. I like mesmerising.
RACHEL   Does it...
MATT   What?
RACHEL   Does it look... I don't know. Weird? Or like... Wrong?
MATT   I think we did a pretty good job tying it.
RACHEL   No, I mean... Nevermind.
MATT   I know this is huge. I get the feeling that there's something you're not telling me, but that doesn't matter. I'm here for whatever you need and when you decide you're ready to talk about it...

Pause. He thinks perhaps she might say something but she doesn't.

MATT   Should I, um, put some music on or something?

She nods. MATT approaches the record collection and peruses. She's not sure how to proceed, then she approaches him, hugging him around the waist.

RACHEL   I need you here. This is really important to me, and I... I'm grateful for everything and how supportive you've been – I'm really happy that you're here.

She kisses him. DAVID enters, provoking RACHEL and MATT to separate. He now wears a collarless white linen shirt.

DAVID   What do you think?
MATT   You look...
RACHEL   Stunning, dazzling, beautiful and mesmerising?
MATT   Yep, exactly.
DAVID   Why, thank you. You look like grandma.

RACHEL smiles. MATT has selected a record and put it on. "Being in Love" by Wet Leg is heard.

DAVID No, turn that off.

MATT You don't like it?

YASH (*From off*) That better not be what I think it is.

DAVID Now look what you've done.

RUTH enters from the hall. She now wears a smart formal black dress or blouse and trousers.

MATT I don't understand.

RUTH Probably best to stop that...

MATT E tu Brute?

RUTH Oh, hush hush. We just don't want –

YASH (*From off*) You come into my house and think you can just make yourself at home, do you?

MATT He's never spoken to me like that before.

DAVID Fear not. He's not talking to you.

MATT hurriedly turns the record off. RUTH sees RACHEL for the first time.

RUTH Oh my.

RACHEL Save it. Matt used all the best adjectives.

RUTH Oh, well. I will say that I am very proud today –

RACHEL Thanks, mum.

RUTH And what about me? Do I pass the test?

RACHEL What test is that?

RUTH The Rachel Singh Diwali excellence test. Your silence isn't very reassuring.

RACHEL It's just that... You're in black.

MATT Black is sort of... A colour to be avoided around this time.

DAVID Does it matter?

He gives RACHEL a warning look. She speaks reluctantly.

RACHEL It's not going to ruin the day.

MATT It's just sort of a superstition, I guess. I mean, all of it is. Including the washing, and –

RACHEL It's not superstition.

MATT No. Tradition...

DAVID Potato, aloo. What's the point of it?

MATT The act of bathing, it's a metaphor that represents when the gods banished demons. It's about washing away the evil from your body which has built up and tempted you.

RACHEL Exactly. So we wash ourselves, and wear new or clean clothes, and we avoid evilness and greed at all costs. Just like the Gods did.

RUTH I'm sure it's a lovely story.

RACHEL It's not a story, Mum. Sorry. It's just, when you say "story", it's a bit diminishing.

RUTH Oh, I really wasn't trying to...

DAVID Has anyone told Grandad he needs to wash today?

RUTH It's difficult for him to get up to the shower without one of us there. Or his carer.

RACHEL That's fine, he doesn't need to.

DAVID But we do?

MATT Maybe you've got more evil that needs to be washed away. I've heard you have to be pretty soulless to work in recruitment. All that jargon and double talk...

DAVID How dare you, Matthew. I am a paragon of –

RACHEL When you're in the position that you're too

weak to climb stairs –

DAVID Alright, we're only having a laugh. Don't get all –

RUTH Kids.

Pause. DAVID, sullen, turns the record back on. "Being in Love" plays from the point it was turned off. RUTH begins to tell him to turn it off again before YASH enters, wearing a Kurta, which he is clearly not used to.

YASH I thought I told you to turn that rubbish off.

DAVID It may surprise you to learn that it's not actually my fault it's playing.

YASH approaches the record player and turns it off.

YASH Yeah, right.

MATT Actually, um… I put it on…

YASH Oh, really? Sorry, Matt, how rude of me.

MATT Quite alright, Yash.

YASH turns back to the record player to put it back on.

DAVID You're ridiculous!

YASH Don't try to twist this –

DAVID What am I twisting exactly? I lovingly buy you a record I think you'll like for Christmas, you couldn't be less grateful. But your precious daughter's boyfriend puts it on…

RUTH That's enough. You know your father is just trying to be polite to our guest. Even if he is being quite inconsiderate at the same time. Now, what's next dear, are we doing the chai tea?

RACHEL It's just chai mum.

RUTH Oh, is it?

RACHEL Yeah, chai means tea, if you say chai tea you're saying the same word twice.

RUTH   I didn't realise.

MATT   Should we do the... P-R-E-S-E-N-T-S?

He whispers and spells out the word.

RACHEL   You know my family can spell, right?

DAVID   Presents?

MATT   Of course, just, um, trying to be... Subtle.

RUTH   You haven't got anything for us, have you?

MATT   Just some little bits...

RACHEL   Let's wait for Grandad, he loves presents.

RUTH   You didn't mention anything about presents, we haven't got anything for you. I'm not prepared!

YASH   We're hosting, isn't that present enough?

DAVID   We could go and get Grandad now, and then do the presents sooner...

RACHEL   That's not the plan.

RUTH   David we've explained-

RACHEL   Besides, I haven't wrapped his present yet.

YASH   Does that matter?

RUTH   Oh he does like opening presents. We could put it in a nice bag or something?

DAVID   Why haven't you done it already?

RACHEL   What? There was a lot –

DAVID   This was the one thing? Isn't it on your stupid little list?

RACHEL   We just thought – Earlier in the week, when he was...

Pause.

YASH   He had a bit of a turn.

RACHEL   We didn't know if he'd be allowed to – If he'd be well enough... So I didn't prioritise...

RUTH　　It's alright.
DAVID　　What kind of a turn did he have?
YASH　　He was ok.
DAVID　　Was he ok, or did he have a turn?
RUTH　　He's fine now, that's the important thing.
DAVID　　But –
RUTH　　Please, David.
RACHEL　　There is one I want to give now, actually.
MATT　　Really?
RACHEL　　Yeah. You know... Something for Dad.

Rachel exits.

YASH　　For me? I always knew I was special.
RUTH　　You don't think it could be... Dear, do you know what day it is today?
YASH　　Apart from Diwali?
RUTH　　Saturday, dear.
YASH　　You mean –

He looks at her, panicked, then jumps up and runs to his record collection. RACHEL re-enters holding a small carrier bag.

RACHEL　　So we'll do the others later but I do have one extra thing for you, Dad.
YASH　　Yes, and I for you.
RACHEL　　You do this every week.
DAVID　　Is someone going to tell me what's going on?
RACHEL　　I wanted to expand my music knowledge and taste range, and when Dad caught me going through his collection –
YASH　　And putting everything back in the wrong place...
RACHEL　　We decided he would recommend records,

once a week on Saturday's. But he seems to forget on a weekly basis.

YASH   Not forget, see. Here.

He approaches and hands her a record – "Soul Mining" by The The.

YASH   Happy?

RACHEL   It's just... I didn't mean for you to just pluck something out at random... I wanted you to select things because they mean something to you.

YASH   Everything in there means something to me.

DAVID has moved over to the record collection, and now pulls out an album by Soft Cell, holding it up.

DAVID   Really? What exactly does "*Non-Stop Erotic Cabaret*" mean to you?

YASH   This is a really iconic –

RACHEL   Forget all the context. Tell me what it makes you feel when you listen to it.

They are all waiting for YASH to speak, but he merely shrugs. She holds the carrier bag out to him.

YASH   What's this?

YASH takes the bag, pulling out a record – "All Things Must Pass" by George Harrison.

RACHEL   You don't already have it, I checked.

YASH   No, I know I don't. Thank you.

RACHEL   I just figured... You've been recommending stuff to me, and I thought I could... Because we were getting presents anyway...

YASH   I must have listened to it at some point, maybe 30 years ago... Recognise the odd song name...

MATT   Not one of the first people you think of when someone says "The Beatles", is he? John, Paul, George... He's always third.

YASH His solo career was quite different to his time in the group. Distinguished, even.

MATT Arguably the biggest band of all time though. You can't escape that. It's like... Daniel Radcliffe, now. No matter how many silly independent films he does, no one is ever not going to see him as Harry Potter?

DAVID Who?

MATT Very funny.

RACHEL But he did escape it. If you listen to what he was doing – in the band... The first songs he wrote by himself, they're so... Tired of what he knows, they're looking for something new. "Within You Without You", "Love You To", they sound so...

YASH You're talking about the sitar. Norwegian Wood too, that's the song that really changed things.

RACHEL Yes, well, no. Not *just* that he was using a sitar –

MATT They're not my favourites.

YASH It was a completely different sound. Revolver, Sgt Pepper, White Album...

MATT Never mind all that. Stick to Yellow Submarine, that's what I say.

YASH That's on Revolver.

MATT Oh.

RACHEL It's not just the sitar... The lyrics, when you listen to them – all about religion and... Doesn't it do something for you? It's western music as eastern as it had ever been heard before. Don't you see what I'm saying?

DAVID It's your heritage. Packaged up for something that your anglicised ears won't find quite so foreign.

RACHEL That's not exactly what I'm... But doesn't

that mean something to you? Something more than Yellow Submarine?

YASH I'll listen to the album. You're right, if you're taking my recommendations...

RACHEL You're not listening to me.

DAVID What a surprise.

YASH Give it a rest, will you? Thank you, Rachel.

DAVID goes to retort, RUTH cuts him off before he can. DAVID subtly turns the Wet Leg record back on, perhaps starting the second song, "Chaise Longue".

RUTH This album does mean something to you. Don't you remember? We went to see The The. It was the first concert you took me to.

MATT Really?

YASH I do remember, actually.

RACHEL How old were you?

YASH Around your age, I imagine.

MATT Wow, you've been together such a long time!

RUTH I hope you're not implying something about my age, young man.

MATT No, sorry, I didn't – Just amazing, that's what I meant. Really amazing.

YASH I was just getting into it all back then.

MATT You weren't into music before that?

YASH Not really, until the mid eighties. I just remember that time... Falling head over heels in love.

MATT So sweet.

RUTH He's referring to the music, dear.

MATT Oh.

YASH Everything I listened to was a new delight. Now everything seems to be... derivative.

RACHEL   What about before that?

YASH   That was the first time I could afford a record player, so –

RACHEL   What about when you were a kid? Didn't you listen to whatever Grandma and Grandad liked?

YASH   That was just a lot of Bollywood musicals Grandma liked, it wasn't for me.

RACHEL   So mum comes along and all of a sudden you're really into all this new stuff. Convenient.

YASH   It had nothing to do with your mother, really.

RUTH   How kind of you to say, darling.

YASH   It was my age of rebellion. Discovering things that I didn't have access to in my childhood.

RACHEL   But you did have –?

YASH   Yes, but... All those flutes and the falsetto singing and... It wasn't anything that made you feel... Made you want to dance. Yes, we used to dance. Come on, Ruth. Let's show these kids how we used to boogie.

DAVID   Please don't say boogie ever again.

RUTH   Can't really dance to this kind of thing.

MATT   You can sort of... Nod your head to the beat.

YASH   Deriv –

DAVID   Oh for god's sake. Stop it.

YASH   Yes, I think I will.

YASH makes a point of turning the record off, which infuriates DAVID.

RUTH   Where did we get to with the tea?

MATT   Oh, that's me!

MATT exits to the hall.

YASH   I'm going to put this one right here, my pile

to listen to.

DAVID There's at least 30 albums in that pile.

YASH And I will get through all of them. Alright? I even listened to this awful –

DAVID Would you stop about the bloody... You're so ungrateful, you know?

YASH Am I?

DAVID It was a Christmas present. From your son. I try to do something nice –

YASH I assumed you were trying to punish me for something.

DAVID It's ok for your favourite child to try and connect with you...

RUTH Your father and I don't have favourites.

DAVID I have to sit here and watch you try to say positive things, when you have no intention of showing me that courtesy.

YASH Stop acting like a child, will you?

RACHEL Don't let him push your buttons, David.

DAVID Stop telling me what to do.

RACHEL I'm not!

RUTH (*Loudly*) I'm looking forward to trying this tea.

DAVID Do we have to?

RACHEL Yes.

RUTH It's good to try new things.

DAVID Why is that?

RUTH It's just a saying, dear.

DAVID No, why do we *have* to try it?

RACHEL Because it's part of the celebration.

DAVID So what? You're being such –

PASSING

RUTH David.

DAVID Why do we have to do everything according to your bloody list? You're being such a dictator. Aren't we supposed to be having fun?

He turns the record back on. 'Wet Dream' plays.

DAVID Come on, mum, let's have a boogie!

Perhaps RUTH half-heartedly tries to appease him, dancing a little. During the below, she turns the record down.

RACHEL I don't care what you think. It's got to be perfect for Grandad.

DAVID Grandad's not even here! Why now? Why, all of a sudden, is it so important that we do all this? All the cleaning ourselves and playing dress up, drinking fucking tea.

RACHEL We can't lose it...

DAVID After all these years that we've ignored this –

RUTH We haven't ignored...

DAVID That we have *not* celebrated... Why is it now so vital that we start doing so?

RACHEL Because.

DAVID Yes?

RACHEL What if it's his last one?

Pause. RACHEL and RUTH look nervously at YASH.

YASH Don't be ridiculous. His last...

DAVID What do you mean?

YASH Why is everyone looking at me?

RUTH Yash...

DAVID What does that mean exactly?

YASH Don't "Yash" me. Don't say my name like that.

RACHEL Dad, I know it's difficult...

DAVID Why is it difficult? What's –?

RUTH Alright, perhaps we should –

YASH Yes. Good idea. No need to sit around – This is a day of celebration, isn't it? Nothing to mope about.

RACHEL We have to face up to...

DAVID Face up to what?

RUTH Dear, the situation –

YASH Stop doing that, Ruth.

DAVID Lay off. She's just trying –

YASH You have no idea what she's trying to do.

RUTH I'm in the room!

RACHEL We have to be realistic about this.

YASH I know that, Rachel! I do understand. Grandad is... He's ill.

DAVID Just how ill?

RUTH David, please. The situation is a little different now from when you last saw your Grandad, alright?

DAVID No, not alright. Different how?

RUTH As people get on in life, their immune systems, they take a little while longer to recover.

YASH But that doesn't mean...

RUTH Of course, dear.

DAVID How worried should we be?

YASH Not – As I have said, there's no need! What? Why are you all looking at me like that?

RACHEL We're not –

YASH I can see it in your – Don't treat me like...

RUTH It's alright, Yash.

PASSING

YASH   No, it's not alright, actually.
RUTH   There's no need to get –
YASH   Who's upset, Ruth?
RACHEL   Please, let's just have a rational conversation!
YASH   Don't patronise me. Do me that courtesy...
RUTH   No one's –
DAVID   Let's go. I want to go see him.
RUTH   David, stop now.
DAVID   If he's really ill –
YASH   For god's sake, he is not –
RUTH   He's recovering...
RACHEL   He is, but let's face it, he hasn't got all the time in the world.
YASH   Rachel...
DAVID   Then I want to –
RUTH   He is not at death's door, he will be here this afternoon David.
DAVID   I don't want to just sit around waiting, pretending –
YASH   Will all of you please –
RACHEL   Dad, come on. I was only saying that Grandad isn't going to be around forever –
YASH   He is not going to die.

In the silence that follows this, the record catches YASH's attention.

YASH   We're not still listening to this shit are we?
RUTH   Yash. Language in front of the children.
YASH   I'm turning it off.
RUTH   Matt put that on...
YASH   There's only so much a man can take.

DAVID See how he treats gifts Rach?

RUTH Just let him –

YASH Just stop. All of you.

Pause. YASH goes over to the record player and carefully removes the record.

YASH "Just let me"... I'm not a bloody – One's elders are to be respected... Parents above all. Do you have any idea what my father would do – And, In my own house... was a time when I could say that a record was a pile of shit, and that meant that it was exactly that. I mean, if my dad said something... It meant something. He'll tell you himself. He'll tell you what he thinks, and you'll listen. And he's going to be around a good long while to do exactly...

Overcome, YASH suddenly lashes out, hitting the record against a table or the wall. It snaps in half. He immediately recovers and regrets this. Silence. RACHEL and RUTH look from him to DAVID nervously. DAVID goes to say something, then turns to leave instead.

RUTH David, wait. It was just an –

DAVID Save it.

RACHEL Why did you do that?

DAVID Yeah. Go on, I'd like to hear an answer to that.

Slight pause. YASH is lost for words, still a little in shock.

YASH (*Muttering*) I need a drink...

Suddenly MATT bursts through the door from the hall, carrying a tray loaded with mugs and cooking pot and ladle.

MATT Right, who's up for some chai tea?

Immediately the atmosphere hits him, and he looks around at each of them awkwardly. His eyes settle pleadingly on RACHEL.

RUTH I think it's just chai, dear.

Slight pause, MATT takes in the scene.

MATT What happened to the music?

Slow fade to black.

ACT ONE, SCENE 2

Lights up. Music should come in loud, then fade and play in the background throughout the scene. It is one of Yash's records, perhaps "Brothers in Arms" by Dire Straits. If so, the act should open with "Money for Nothing", just after the intro to the song, where the guitar comes in.

The living room as before. RUTH flits around, tidying up what little mess there is. DAVID sits holding a mug. YASH is opening and pouring a bottle of beer with as much precision as is possible.

DAVID *(To YASH)* Moving on from tea?

YASH I liked it.

RUTH takes the mugs out to the hall. YASH finishes pouring his beer.

YASH *(To himself)* Perfect.

DAVID You want more head than that.

YASH I know what I like. If I say it's perfect...

DAVID Surprised you lasted this long.

He drinks, a big gulp.

YASH Needed more head.

RUTH returns and begins dusting with a cloth.

DAVID When's Grandad getting here?

RUTH As you know, we're picking him up later.
DAVID When is later, exactly?
YASH At a time subsequent to the present.
DAVID Did anyone ask you?
YASH I believe you spoke to the room in general.
DAVID Your belief was incorrect.

Silence. RUTH gives YASH a look.

YASH What?
RUTH Don't you have something to say?
YASH Nothing specific.
RUTH Something to your son?
YASH What do you want me to say?
RUTH Perhaps an apology?
YASH He doesn't want to hear empty words.
RUTH Why don't you try words that aren't blooming empty then, dear?
YASH Blooming, Ruth?
DAVID Mum, can you not swear in front of me please.

Pause. The humour between YASH and DAVID at RUTH's expense quickly fades back to sullen silence.

DAVID Can't we just go get grandad now?
RUTH We cannot.
DAVID I just want to see that he's ok.
YASH He just wants to speed things up so he can run off back to his flat. Catalogue all of this as more bad parenting he can resent us for.
RUTH Rather dramatic, dear.
YASH You know, son, one day I won't be around anymore. And you'll be sat here with your thoughts

that really should have been spoken, and your... But of course it'll be too late by then. So all you'll really have are the broken pieces of a vinyl and the sense that you should have tried harder to put it back together.

With a swig, he finishes off his drink.

DAVID   Why don't you have another drink, Dad.

YASH   I most certainly will.

He exits to the hall, crossing RACHEL and MATT who enter, jovially.

RUTH   Everything clean?

MATT   Spotless.

RACHEL   Tidy.

DAVID   Didn't do anything in my room did you?

RACHEL   That was your responsibility.

DAVID   We were kept quite busy in here, actually.

MATT   I would wager you haven't moved since we left.

RUTH   You would win that bet.

RACHEL   Thank you, Mum, it looks great.

YASH has returned, pouring a beer rather clumsily, so that there is a lot of froth.

DAVID   Too much head.

RACHEL   He knows what he likes. "If I say it's perfect..."

YASH   Would anyone care to join me in a beverage?

MATT   I couldn't possibly refuse.

YASH   Excellent. Here, you have this one...

RACHEL   Dad. Stop it, he's too polite to say no.

MATT   I don't mind...

YASH   No, quite right. No one deserves this. Anyone else?

RUTH Don't have any more.

YASH I'm fine.

RACHEL It's just because you have to go pick up Grandad.

YASH It's two beers, would everyone calm down?

MATT It'll be out of his system in a couple of hours.

YASH Thank you. Now. You'll be pleased with me when you see what I've got.

He exits to the hall.

RACHEL It's alright, Mum, let him have one more.

RUTH It is a special occasion.

RACHEL That stuff is important today.

MATT Beer's always important, isn't it?

RACHEL I just mean... Today is about new beginnings, and generosity –

RUTH Are we doing it all right, do you think?

MATT We're not doing all the traditions, but I'd say we can be pretty pleased with what we've achieved so far, right Rach?

YASH returns, holding more bottles of beer. Some of the brands among them are Cobra and Kingfisher.

YASH Look at these!

RACHEL Very impressive, Dad.

YASH Right? Now try to tell me I'm not getting into the spirit of things... Cheers everyone.

They all toast with the beers YASH has handed around.

MATT It's funny though, that we're not doing some of the spiritual things...

RACHEL We talked about it, remember? I didn't want to push my luck with what you'd all tolerate.

MATT Yeah, I know. I just mean because the prayer

is probably the most important aspect of the whole day.

DAVID   Pretty sure someone told me the lights were the most important thing.

MATT   They go hand in hand. All of it does. The washing, and cleaning and the lighting of candles and the pooja.

YASH   Pooja, that's the... Prayer?

MATT   That's right. The Lakshmi Pooja, prayer to the goddess of prosperity.

RACHEL   You must remember. Grandma used to talk about it. She used to pray. She'd try to explain it but she'd lapse into Hindi.

YASH   Of course. I do. It's all just sort of faded... All so many years ago now.

RACHEL   That's a bit sad, isn't it?

RUTH   You have to take into account... Grandma and Grandad, they never pushed anything on your father. They wouldn't force you, if you weren't interested –

YASH   No, they weren't like that, especially dad. It was my mum that was more into all of this. If you ask Grandad what this whole thing's about, he'd probably just tell you they set off fireworks. That's all he remembers.

RUTH   Don't be silly, dear. I'm sure he could tell you loads –

RACHEL   But back then... You used to celebrate in India didn't you, as a child?

RUTH   He was so young then.

RACHEL   Right but, didn't you... I don't know, think it was special? All of this? Everything they brought over with them, that you brought over?

YASH   It wasn't what I cared about, I was 6!

Everyone at my school looked different, I just wanted to fit in and talk about football and superhero comic books.

RUTH　　There wasn't a big Indian community here back then.

YASH　　I didn't want anything to do with it, I just wanted to be a good little British boy. All those gods with the multiple arms and elephant heads, I've never been able to remember the names.

RACHEL　　You don't remember anything?

YASH　　No, I do... Odd things. Dad in the garden setting up the fireworks and making those... Things with the coloured rice? And the food... Puris and curry, and... Mum's papadums, so oily and crispy and greasy. Like nothing... Not like these flimsy ones you get in restaurants nowadays.

Slight pause. RACHEL seems unsatisfied. MATT fills the silence.

MATT　　That's exactly what celebrations like this are all about. Memories, traditions, passed down... Personal family traditions. It's a warm feeling, the nostalgia of it. It is just like Christmas, really. You can still eat a massive roast dinner and put presents under a tree, and do all the other little things that your family, and no other family, does every year... Without remembering to celebrate that Jesus was born. And today, you can still light the candles. It's still the festival of lights, just because you don't do the pooja.

Slight pause. DAVID sees an opportunity.

DAVID　　It's not really 'just like Christmas' though, is it?

MATT　　Well, I just meant, in the sense –

DAVID　　I mean, anyone can celebrate Christmas, can't they.

RACHEL Where are you going with this?

MATT If they're not Christian, you mean?

DAVID Right, no one's going to blink at a British family – any family – celebrating Christmas in this country.

MATT I don't see why they would...

DAVID But this is a bit different, isn't it?

RACHEL David.

DAVID Maybe not if we'd been doing this year on year, all our lives, but this is our first time.

RACHEL It wouldn't be different.

DAVID No? This day has never meant anything to us before now.

RACHEL Yes it has. Maybe not to you, but to our family.

DAVID Our family? Really? The family in this room?

YASH What the hell are you getting at?

DAVID I guess I'm just wondering... Do we really have the right to be doing all this?

RACHEL Of course we do. We should have been –

DAVID I'm just making the point that... Well, ok to give an example, let's say Matt here... If Matt decided of his own accord that he wanted to throw a Diwali party – For argument's sake let's say he did it without Rachel... I just wonder, no matter how much preparation and research he did, if he threw that Diwali party... wouldn't that be...

YASH Spit it out will you.

RACHEL He's saying it would be cultural appropriation.

MATT Woah, ok. But you get that's not what I'm

– This isn't my –
YASH What? Why would it?
RUTH Matt can have a party, can't he? I don't see what harm it does...
RACHEL We don't have time to get into the minutia of this issue.
DAVID Maybe we should, though.
RUTH It's just a bit of fun –
RACHEL Mum, it's not just 'a bit of fun', you can't say –
YASH I don't see why anyone can't just have a go if they want...
MATT Well, not anyone.
RUTH Because we also do Christmas? Is it a one or the other type of thing?
YASH Because we're British, is it?
DAVID Yes, that. But not just that.
RUTH Because – what? Hang on, so are we not doing Diwali anymore?
RACHEL No, we absolutely are.
DAVID But should we...?
RACHEL You know it's different. We can.
DAVID But can we?
YASH Anyone can! Anyone who can master that bloody tea.
RUTH Is it because we haven't done it before?
MATT Can I just say, I would never, ever –
YASH Do you mean he can't because he's white?
DAVID Ding ding ding.
RACHEL (*To DAVID*) Why are you doing this right now?
MATT I know I helped with the tea and everything,

but on my own I wouldn't dream of –
RACHEL   It's completely different.
RUTH   Why is it different?
RACHEL   Because, mum. We're –
DAVID   But are we?
RACHEL   Stop doing that.
RUTH   I don't understand.
YASH   Surely it makes no difference whether –
RACHEL   Yes, it does. Of course it makes a difference, because we're owed this.
RUTH   Why is it different? We're all white.

Slight pause.

RUTH   Except Dad.
RACHEL   We're mixed race, Mum.
DAVID   But even so –
RACHEL   I think you've made your point.
YASH   What, so because your skin tone is a touch darker...
DAVID   Not sure I have just yet.
YASH   You two live in the same country, the same county... What's the difference? I don't see why Matt –
RACHEL   He can do whatever he bloody likes.
MATT   But I wouldn't...
YASH   Just because of a bit of a tan.
RACHEL   I'm sorry, a bit of a tan?
YASH   To look at the two of you kids, you might not even know you weren't just European.
DAVID   A lot of people assume I'm Turkish for some reason.
RACHEL   It's not about the colour of anyone's skin.

DAVID No, I'm saying it's about our family specifically.

YASH It's just a bloody party...

MATT Well, you have to consider how much respect there is. Is it appropriation or just appreciation?

DAVID Matthew's hit the nail on the head there. And because we have never been bothered about this before, isn't it just as bad for us to be...

He trails off, seeing RACHEL's defeated look. Slight pause. RACHEL is quiet when she speaks, as if she is just speaking to DAVID.

RACHEL You know it's different. I see what you're trying to do. And you're right, we've never done it before, and we're mixed race we're not... Fully... But we're also not just – We are Indian, Dad is, and our grandparents. We're not taking something that doesn't belong to us. Just something that we never had a chance to experience before, we were never offered. Something that got lost...

Slight pause. Then RACHEL gets up and makes to leave.

MATT Where are you –?

RACHEL I'm fine, I'm fine. I just want to get something.

MATT Rach, wait!

They exit. YASH stands too, heading for the kitchen.

YASH Well. You really know how to clear a room, don't you?

He exits. Silence between DAVID and RUTH.

DAVID Don't give me that look. The Mum look.

RUTH That's just my face, darling.

DAVID Someone needs to ask the big questions, find out why we're doing all of this. I mean, what good is any of this doing anyone?

RUTH What harm is it doing?

Slight pause.

DAVID So. Is he... Um...

RUTH Why don't you ask him?

DAVID That's likely.

RUTH You know he didn't mean to break your record.

DAVID I don't think I *know* that.

RUTH It was an accident.

DAVID Seemed pretty deliberate to me.

RUTH He just gets a little worked up when it comes to Grandad. He's been under an incredible amount of stress, seeing his Dad like that.

DAVID Is that why you're helping out so much?

RUTH Of course.

DAVID But he's not your dad.

RUTH He's family. You don't know what it's been like for everyone. Rachel and your father, they've been...

DAVID Just how bad is he?

RUTH He has good days...

DAVID And bad?

RUTH Yes. Those can be a little scary. He is getting on now, that's just what happens. Some days he can't walk so well, he refuses to eat...

DAVID I should see him more. Is he alright, mum?

RUTH Grandad's going to be fine, you'll see for yourself.

DAVID No, is – Is he alright?

DAVID indicates towards the kitchen.

RUTH He's struggling. Obviously. So, just... Cut him some slack. Rachel too. This is the last time I'm going to ask. Please.

DAVID That's all I seem to have to do around here. Cut people slack, give people breaks.

RUTH That's how family works, dear. Aren't you grateful I'm cutting you some slack for the fuss you just caused?

MATT enters sheepishly.

MATT I was... Um... Sent back in here.

DAVID What's she doing?

MATT Just looking for something. I'm not really sure... It's not on her list, so...

YASH re-enters, holding more bottles of beer.

YASH Nothing wrong with a bit of improvisation.

RUTH I hope we haven't all given a bad impression today. It's not always like this...

DAVID It is.

MATT You should see my family when we get everyone together.

RUTH I'm sure there aren't quite so many arguments.

MATT That's just how relatives show they love each other.

DAVID Nothing breaks your spirit does it?

YASH I would steer well clear, if I had the choice. After all this, to still be thinking about – What?

He has reacted to RUTH glaring at him suddenly.

MATT Thinking about what?

YASH Well, just... Any thoughts you might have about...

DAVID She's not going to like this.
YASH Things moving in a more serious direction.
Slight pause. They all watch MATT.
YASH As you mentioned...
MATT Did I?
YASH This morning –
RUTH Perhaps you wrongfully inferred.
YASH No, I don't believe I did.
MATT I'm not sure what impression I gave...
DAVID Sounds like all of this has put you off.
MATT What? No, nothing's put me off, nothing's changed.
YASH Good, then. This is a cause for celebration.
RUTH Celebration of what?
YASH Of the fantastic news.
RUTH What news is that, dear?
YASH Rachel is moving in with Matt.
MATT Hang on a second...
RUTH Where on earth have you pulled that from?
YASH He said, nothing's changed.
RUTH And you took that to mean they were moving in together?
YASH Yes, because he told me earlier –
MATT I'm not sure what you think I said this morning...
YASH I don't think you said anything, I heard you say –
MATT This really is a discussion you should probably have with Rachel.
YASH Yes, let's get her in here. Rachel!

MATT I meant –

RUTH Some other time.

MATT I'm not saying you're incorrect...

RUTH You don't have to justify anything, dear, I'm sure he's just mistaken.

YASH Why assume that, Ruth?

MATT Maybe you just misinterpreted...

RUTH Misunderstood.

YASH In plain English, you told me that you and Rachel planned to move in together.

MATT No, I definitely –

YASH That is what you said. Why deny it?

MATT Even if I had said... I wouldn't definitively say we planned to do anything... Even if I wanted to...

YASH You do want to?

MATT Well, of co – But, but... Regardless of how I feel...

YASH You're saying Rachel doesn't feel the same?

MATT We've not talked about it...

RUTH If she doesn't feel ready to – quite yet... How did you say it earlier, she's not ready to be a little bird?

DAVID To leave the nest, mum.

MATT I am going to talk to her. I'm planning to. At some point.

DAVID He's unsure now. Something about today has put him off.

RUTH No. That's not true, is it?

MATT Of course –

DAVID Of course!

MATT – not. Of course not, is what I was trying to say.

PASSING

YASH So. You haven't spoken to Rachel about any of this?

MATT We haven't had that conversation... It's just... A sensitive time, and I don't want to spring anything on Rachel while her concentrations are... Elsewhere.

YASH I don't understand.

RUTH Yes you do. It's the wrong time.

RACHEL enters quietly. She is carrying a box of the game Cluedo.

YASH Why is it?

MATT Because of how Rach can be, sometimes.

DAVID How can she be?

MATT Just a bit...

They are all silent. Rachel shakes the box.

RACHEL Anyone for a game?

DAVID Oh no, not fucking Clu –

RUTH Wonderful idea. Just what we need.

They all begin to clear the table, taking used glasses away, making space etc. RACHEL and MATT speak privately.

RACHEL (*To MATT*) Aren't you going to ask me if I'm ok?

MATT Did you hear? I didn't mean –

RACHEL I'd like to know how you were going to finish that sentence. "Just a bit" what?

MATT Rach...

RACHEL I'm joking. It's fine, honestly. I'm fine.

MATT Can we just talk for a minute?

RACHEL Later. Let's just... Let's do this. Who's who then?

YASH I'm going to win. I always win this game.

DAVID   Professor Plum.

RACHEL   Miss Scarlet for me. Dad, Reverend Green? Mum... Mrs White?

RUTH   Custard, please.

RACHEL   Mustard, Mum. Colonel Mustard.

DAVID   Which leaves...

RACHEL   Miss Peacock.

MATT   The role I was born to play.

They gather and settle at the table. RACHEL unpacks the box, with lots of small scraps of paper.

YASH   Roll to see who goes first.

MATT   What's with all these bits of paper?

RUTH   We lost one of the cards years ago so we decided just to write all of them out again, so they would still be identical.

RACHEL   There's one missing... The billiard room, I think.

DAVID   Do we need it?

RUTH   I think we have to play with all the rooms, dear. What if someone wants to go in there?

RACHEL   Right, or if it's the murder room.

DAVID   This feels like the murder room.

RACHEL   The room where the murder takes place.

DAVID   Fine, just write that one again then. Here... This is already taking too long.

DAVID has quickly written on another bit of scrap paper. RACHEL deals out cards and prepares the game.

MATT   Shouldn't we wait for your Grandad to play this? He likes games, doesn't he?

RACHEL   We'll play something else when he gets here.

YASH   Who rolled the highest?

MATT I rolled a six...

YASH Start with you then, and go clockwise.

He rolls the dice, and begins moving his counter.

YASH Go on, go on, move. You can get into the Billiard Room.

RACHEL Why do we play this?

DAVID My question exactly.

RUTH What do you mean, you wanted to play this?

RACHEL No, I mean. Like, originally. Why did we start playing it?

RUTH We've been playing this since before you were born.

MATT It does look like a classic edition.

DAVID That's the polite way of saying it's in terrible condition.

YASH You're right. Just look at the rope. We lost it years ago, this is just a bit of shoelace.

DAVID The lead piping is a Lego piece.

RUTH What did you mean, Rach?

RACHEL I mean... Why did you play this? Of all the games.

RUTH I suppose because your father likes to think he's good at it.

YASH I am.

RACHEL But –

RACHEL continues to question YASH as DAVID tries to instruct MATT. Failing to concentrate, YASH jumps in and out of both conversations.

YASH We have plenty of old games. There's a monopoly set just about as beaten up as this, a chess board somewhere...

RACHEL Right, but all those games...

RUTH What are you trying to say?

RACHEL Like, did you play them as a kid?

Beat.

RUTH (*to YASH*) Rachel's asked you a question.

YASH What? It's not her turn.

RACHEL Not in the game, Dad.

YASH Well, can it wait?

RACHEL Dad. Listen.

YASH What do you want?

RACHEL This game, did you play it as a kid? Or any other games?

YASH Every child plays games, Rachel.

RACHEL This game, though. Did you play this game?

DAVID Are you going?

MATT I have to make an accusation, right? Ok, so... The dagger, I guess?

YASH In order. Please.

MATT Huh?

DAVID You've gotta say it in the right order.

MATT What order?

YASH Blank with the blank in the blank.

MATT Blank?

DAVID Who are you accusing?

MATT Mrs White?

DAVID Ok, then...

MATT In the Billiard Room! Right? Because I'm in there...

DAVID Very good. But... Blank, *with the blank*, first. The weapon.

MATT With the dagger...

DAVID Ok.

MATT Ok?

DAVID Yes. So, all together?

MATT Mrs White, with the dagger, in the Billiard Room.

YASH Probably, I don't know.

DAVID Was that so hard?
MATT Yes.
YASH Hang on, hang on. I missed it, say it again.
DAVID Try to concentrate.
YASH Rachel was –
RUTH Leave him be. We're lucky he's sat still this long.
MATT Mrs. White.
YASH Mrs. White.
MATT Dagger.
YASH Right.
MATT Billiard Room.
YASH Got it.
MATT Ok.

They all look at DAVID.

DAVID What?
RUTH Do you have any of those?
DAVID What were they? Kidding, kidding. I do not.
RACHEL What other games did you play?
DAVID Drop it, will you? We're playing the game you chose.
YASH Cards. We played cards a lot – Hearts I think.
RUTH I don't have any of those, dear.
YASH Poker, gin rummy...
DAVID Dad –
RACHEL All those games, you played them with your school friends? Who introduced you to them?
YASH How am I –?
DAVID Dad, it's your turn to answer.

YASH Hang on, what did Mum say?

DAVID She didn't have any.

RACHEL Think Dad, where did all those games come from? Why do we play this and not...

RUTH You used to play chess with Grandad, didn't you?

YASH Yes, my dad taught me how to play.

RACHEL Really? I never knew that.

YASH She said no to all of them?

DAVID Come on, Dad.

YASH It's a no from me too.

RACHEL It's funny isn't it... Of all the things, that he taught you to play chess.

RUTH It's your turn, dear.

RACHEL Didn't you learn, I don't know... Anything closer to home?

YASH What specifically —?

RACHEL What did you play before chess? You must have stories of living in India as a child, the stuff you did there?

YASH Well, yes. I suppose... Probably.

RUTH Of course he does.

RACHEL But you never talk about it.

RUTH Your father tends to forget.

YASH I do not —

RACHEL You've never passed any of those stories on... We know nothing about that period of your life.

RUTH I've heard a few things over the years.

DAVID Rach if you don't answer —

RACHEL Chill out. I don't have any.

Pause.

DAVID Can you repeat that?

RACHEL What? I don't have any.

YASH You don't have Mrs White, the dagger, or the Billiard Room?

RACHEL No. Why is that such... Oh.

Another pause. They all begin writing frantically, except MATT.

MATT What am I missing here?

DAVID Rachel didn't have any of those cards.

MATT Right...?

DAVID And neither did I... Or Mum or Dad...

MATT I see.

DAVID This just got rather exciting.

RACHEL Why do we play this? Seriously, David complains non-stop. Mum despises it.

RUTH I admit it's not my favourite.

DAVID I'm not complaining now. This is the best this game's ever been. Your turn, Rach.

RACHEL Aren't there any games from your childhood that aren't *Cluedo* or Chess or *Monopoly* or –

YASH Oh, Rachel. Cards, like I said...

RACHEL Games that Grandma taught you.

DAVID Right. I'm rolling for you.

MATT Let her do it.

DAVID You try getting her to concentrate.

YASH Grandma loved to play... gin rummy.

RACHEL Seriously?

DAVID I'm going to assume you want to go into the library...

RACHEL Is that what we've got left of Grandma?

That's it?
RUTH There's no need to get –
RACHEL I'm not getting upset.
RUTH Let's not argue...

RACHEL Can't you see that it's frustrating... Not just that, it's – harrowing, in a way – That's what we have to show for Grandma's life for the woman who moved here to start a whole new life. Instead of remembering and celebrating what this amazing woman brought with her... We just remember the fact that she embraced gin rummy?

DAVID No one's arguing, mum.
RUTH Yes, I know you're not. For once!
YASH Rachel, please...
DAVID Your words hurt, you know.
RUTH Hush, we're all listening to...
DAVID Are we?
YASH We can never just play a game...

RUTH Rachel, that's enough now. We can talk about this some other time. We'd be happy to. Right now, we're doing this, which is what you asked us to do.
RACHEL Fine. Where am I?
MATT The library.
RACHEL I don't want to go to the library.
DAVID Move wherever the hell you like then. You rolled a seven.
RACHEL I don't remember rolling –
YASH What is your accusation, Rachel?
RACHEL Just thinking.
DAVID Take as much time as you need. No really, as

PASSING

much time...

RUTH Yash...

YASH What?

RUTH I don't want to further distract from the game...

YASH What is it?

RUTH You just leant forward.

YASH Yes...?

RUTH When you lean like that, you put your cards out in front... Directly in front of my face.

YASH You cheated?

DAVID Mum!

RUTH I didn't cheat. I didn't mean to see.

MATT Do we have to start again?

YASH No. Nonsense.

DAVID How much did you see?

RUTH Oh... Not... Well, it's just...

YASH Yes?

RUTH Now I'm not saying this to cause any sort of argument.

DAVID Go on.

RUTH Well, when you leant forward... I saw one of your cards was... The Billiard Room.

DAVID Dad!

YASH What? Don't be ridiculous. Show me where. Point to which of these cards is –

RUTH That one.

YASH That doesn't say Billiard Room.

RUTH No? What does it say then?

YASH It's difficult to make it out exactly.

RUTH What do you think it says?

YASH I couldn't tell. I assumed maybe the writer was possibly trying to write... Board Room.

RUTH What?

DAVID Are you out of your mind?

MATT There's no Board Room on the... Um, board.

YASH Isn't there?

DAVID What kind of house would have a board room?

MATT To be fair, what kind of house has a Billiard Room...

DAVID I bet I can find you more houses with billiard rooms than bloody board rooms.

YASH What kind of houses have murders take place in them? What kind of a host invites prospective murderers for dinner, all of whom happen to have a surname that's a different colour? If you start questioning the game, everything falls apart...

DAVID If you start making up rooms, everything falls apart!

YASH The paper quite clearly says –

DAVID Oh so now it's quite clear? A minute ago you were assuming –

RACHEL This is such a ridiculous argument.

YASH Quite right. We can bring this back...

RACHEL What's the point?

YASH No, it'll be easy. Look.

RUTH I don't think you can –

DAVID Why are you moving Rachel?

YASH I'm going back to Matt's turn, to fix this.

DAVID You can't just –

YASH Matt asked for...

MATT Mrs White, Dagger, Billiard room.

RACHEL How did it happen?

RUTH Rachel, dear...

RACHEL I just want to know what happened.

RUTH Your father's trying to figure out his mistake, he doesn't need distracting.

YASH I did not make a mistake.

RACHEL How did everything brought over get completely lost?

YASH He would have asked the question. You would have said you didn't have any. Mum would have said –

DAVID You can't just rewind –

YASH Look, I've fixed it. When the question got round to me, I would have shown him this card.

MATT The board room?

DAVID It's the bloody billiard room.

RUTH Alright, language, please.

YASH And that would have been the end of his turn. Now Rachel would roll –

DAVID That doesn't solve anything!

YASH Your turn, Rachel.

RACHEL Why don't we have anything to show for...

DAVID But we all know that you have that card now.

YASH That doesn't matter.

DAVID Of course it does!

RACHEL This isn't about the games.

YASH No, it isn't. What on earth have you been going on about all this time? Can't you see we're in the middle –

RACHEL It's about having Christmas and not Diwali. Pigs in blankets and not chaats. It's about dresses and not saris. Learning French and not Hindi. Piano lessons and not the sitar. Listening to The The and not Bollywood musicals.

It's about George Harrison being the closest thing to our heritage that we can stand. It's about not having a statue of Ganesh. And yes, that's the one with the head of an elephant. Why do we have to clarify that?

DAVID I don't know how you have the patience...

RUTH I always say... Games bring out the worst in people. Matt, I hope you don't think –

MATT Oh, please don't worry...

RUTH puts her hand up and waits to be called on like she's at school.

YASH Rachel. Now I've –

DAVID Whose turn is it now?

MATT Sorry I'm just trying to listen –

YASH What has that got to do with –

RACHEL We don't have any indicators in our lives of the fact that we're Indian. Even the colour of our skin doesn't necessarily –

YASH This is irrelevant.

RACHEL Why don't we have more of what should have been passed down?

YASH If you won't have your turn –

DAVID You put those dice down.

RACHEL Forget the stupid game!

DAVID You can't just throw all the rules out the window.

YASH I can do whatever I like.

DAVID No you absolutely –

YASH slaps the table loudly, stopping everyone.

YASH We're just trying to play a nice family game, and the two of you –

RUTH Yash, there's no need...

YASH Perhaps there is need, Ruth. In other households, children listen to their parents. Now I am going to roll the dice, if no one else will have their go.

DAVID No, what?

RACHEL Why won't you listen to me!

YASH Oh look. Double six.

DAVID You can't use that, what the hell are you doing!

RUTH Alright everyone...

RACHEL Dad, look at me.

DAVID Don't you dare move that counter.

RACHEL What if it's too late and we lose it all forever?

YASH One, two...

DAVID Stop!

DAVID goes to grab YASH's counter from his hand, and the two struggle over it, across the board. RACHEL's words are lost on them, with only MATT struggling to pay attention.

RACHEL What if we lose Grandad, and everything that came over with them goes with him?

The arguments continue, DAVID demanding YASH fighting over a board piece and RACHEL fighting for their attention, until:

RUTH That's it!

With one swift movement, RUTH flips the game board, sending pieces flying. A moment of silence, as they all react in shock. Blackout.

ACT II, SCENE 1

Lights up. The scene is exactly as it was at the end of the previous act, the board overturned, game pieces all over the room. Complete silence, which the characters seem to be waiting for RUTH to break. She stares blankly, but after a moment a smile comes across her face. She fails to stifle a giggle.

RUTH   Sorry. It's serious. Sorry.

They all look at her, unsure. She continues to chuckle.

RUTH   Sorry.

RACHEL   It's alright, Mum.

RUTH   It's funny.

DAVID   It is?

RUTH   It's just so ludicrous. Can you imagine? Flipping the board.

DAVID   Don't have to imagine...

RUTH   In front of guests!

MATT   I'm hardly a guest now I've seen a famous Singh family board flip!

DAVID   Oh you've heard this happens?

MATT   It's legendary throughout the land.

RUTH   It did use to be a staple of kid's childhood. Come to think of it, that's probably how we lost the lead piping... At least this time you're all still here to help me tidy up.

DAVID   We're not playing again then?

YASH   Don't be ridiculous.

PASSING

They all start to move around the room, gathering up the pieces and packing away.

RUTH   I'm glad we did all of that. Makes a nice memory, doesn't it? One we'll never forget, at least. Right, Rachel, what's next then?

RACHEL   Um. I don't know where my list's gone.

RUTH   Should probably put the oven on. Shall we? Start getting all that food ready. Yash, more drinks for everyone? David will you put this away?

RUTH exits to the hall.

MATT   She seemed... In high spirits...

RACHEL   Nothing like ruining a board game to make you feel elated.

DAVID   Mum didn't ruin it.

YASH (*Exiting*) Don't start. I did not cheat –

RACHEL   Let's leave it now.

DAVID continues to pack away the game. MATT tries to speak to RACHEL subtly, out of DAVID's earshot.

MATT   Rach, look – What you heard before... I wasn't trying to say –

RACHEL   Matt, let's not... I should go see if –

MATT   Don't run away, please.

DAVID   That's what we do in this family, Matt. Run away after a fight and pretend nothing happened.

RACHEL   Can you not eavesdrop?

DAVID   Can you not try to have a private conversation when I'm in the room? Thank you.

They all wait as DAVID finishes putting the game away and carries it offstage.

RACHEL   I don't want to fight. I don't want to be angry –

MATT Neither do – I know you said later, just... I'm sorry.

RACHEL I know you are.

MATT And you're not... Obviously. You're not... Anything, I don't even know what I was trying to say. This is all amazing. And I'm so lucky.

RACHEL This isn't a good time for you to start rambling.

MATT Right, and I get that –

RACHEL Matt. Let's get through this day, ok? Please?

RUTH enters suddenly and loudly, carrying with her a large photo album. YASH and DAVID follow sheepishly – or perhaps RUTH ushers them into the room ahead of her.

RUTH Right. Oven is on, snacks are in. Hope everyone is hungry.

DAVID Starving, actually.

RACHEL What have you got there, mum?

RUTH I was just thinking. It's so lovely remembering all those times we've played games as a family – the good and the bad times. It occurred to me that Matt has missed so much, he might be interested in seeing it all, through the years.

MATT I absolutely would.

RACHEL What? Mum! No.

RUTH If we have time to fit it in, Rachel?

RACHEL We actually don't have time, sorry.

RUTH Oh come on, just a quick look. The journey of how you came to be the amazing girl you are today, immortalised in this book.

MATT I would love to see.

RACHEL What are you doing to me?

RUTH Nothing to be embarrassed about.

RACHEL I doubt that.

RUTH Oh, no. I've left my glasses in the kitchen, could you, Matt –?

MATT I'm on it.

RUTH They're just on the side I think...

RACHEL smiles reassuringly at MATT as he exits to the hall. RUTH watches him go, then her jovial demeanour fades instantly. She speaks in a threatening whisper.

RUTH Now I'm going to say this quickly, quietly, and only once. So pay attention. We will have no more arguments of that sort in front of company, is that understood? Discussions are allowed, encouraged even. But as soon as they turn nasty... Lets just say that the game board isn't the only thing I'll be flipping over.

DAVID You're going to flip... Us?

RUTH Don't test me. Come on, now. We don't need to argue just because we're all together for once.

RACHEL Sorry, mum.

RUTH That's alright, Rachel. Is everyone else sorry?

DAVID Oh, absolutely.

RUTH Yash?

YASH Yes? Sorry.

RUTH Good. Now, no more arguments. Everyone clear?

DAVID To be honest, I'm still a bit confused about the flipping part...

RUTH waves to shush DAVID as MATT enters, holding RUTH's glasses case, which he hands to her.

MATT Smells good in there!

RUTH Oh, good, good we can get started. Come sit

next to me. And what a way to begin. Oh my.

MATT Oh man, is that –?

RACHEL What?

RUTH Yes, yes!

YASH She wasn't an attractive baby.

RACHEL Dad!

MATT It's a cute, um... Hat... That you're wearing.

RACHEL That's all you can manage?

MATT Your face is very... Very round.

RUTH Moonface Rachel, yes.

DAVID Amazing.

RACHEL Would you stop? Don't we have more important things to be –

DAVID Hush now, Moonface. Everyone's enjoying picture time.

MATT Oh this one's nice. You're dressed up as a... A bear I think?

RUTH A squirrel.

YASH Ah yes, I remember. For the nativity.

DAVID We all remember the famous squirrel present in the barn at the birth of Jesus.

MATT And here, a cowboy? Aw and then Santa.

RUTH We had a phase of dressing her up when she was small, putting hats on her.

YASH To lessen the effect of the circular head.

RACHEL Honestly, this is –

RUTH Don't worry darling, you grew out of it.

RACHEL Oh good. I'm so glad I don't have to think about which hat I'm going to wear when I dress myself.

DAVID Maybe you should.

RUTH One with Grandma and Grandad.

RACHEL looks at YASH, who avoids her gaze.

RACHEL Grandma's in a sari, and I'm wearing jeans.

MATT Very small, cute little jeans.

DAVID You can't put a baby in a sari Rach, lighten up.

YASH Maybe a turban though.

They look at him.

YASH To hide the effect of the head.

MATT Who's this?

RUTH That's Rachel's favourite teacher, Mr Higgins.

MATT You're only about four in this photo?

RUTH Five, I think. He taught you for Year 1.

DAVID Your favourite ever teacher was the one you had in Year 1?

RACHEL Never really liked any of the ones I had after that.

MATT There were a few good ones.

RUTH Look, here she is when she moved school, where she would've met – Oh, yes. There. Who's that handsome young man? Even at such a young age, you were very smartly dressed and presentable.

MATT Thank you.

YASH Who knew back then, one day we'd be sitting here?

RACHEL Not me, I thought boys were gross. Especially you with your pocket protractor set.

MATT You never know when you'll need to measure an angle on the fly.

RUTH Here you are again, these are just class

photos for a while.

DAVID I recognise him.

MATT That's Mr Davies, I really liked him. Physics teacher.

RACHEL You liked Davies? He was the worst of the lot.

DAVID He was ok, wasn't he? They all blur...

MATT What did you not like about him?

RACHEL He had his favourites, you were probably one of them.

RUTH You were every teachers' favourite I expect.

RACHEL And if you weren't one of the chosen few...

MATT What?

RACHEL Well, he picked on people.

YASH He picked on you?

MATT I don't remember that.

RACHEL Of course you don't.

MATT Sorry?

RUTH This one's good. The only time she made it onto a sports team.

DAVID She wasn't even any good at hockey, she was just the only one that would wear the smelly goalie pads.

YASH In what way did he pick on you?

RACHEL Little things.

YASH Such as?

RACHEL Leave it, Dad.

RUTH And here, look, another one of the two of you –

MATT Is that one of those awful discos?

DAVID How come you're wearing a suit and the rest

of the kids are in jeans and t-shirts?

MATT Dress to impress.

YASH I'm starting to remember this man.

RUTH Which, dear?

YASH This Mr. Davies.

RACHEL Dad.

YASH Is this the one...

RUTH That fateful parents evening.

YASH Yes, yes!

RACHEL Oh, please don't.

MATT What happened?

RUTH You remember those parents evenings you had, with the teachers all sat at their little tables, and we had to go round to each one and hear about how well –

YASH Or how badly –

RUTH Yes, or how poorly, you had been doing at school.

YASH Right, and on this occasion – it was Rachel's parents evening. We'd sat down with this guy – Mr Davies. As I recall, it hadn't been the most impressive night up to that point.

RACHEL Alright!

YASH You ended up doing very well, we're all very proud etcetera... But at this time, Physics was not one of the subjects that we had high hopes for...

RACHEL You make me sound like a complete failure.

YASH We were expecting another stern face, that's the main point. But we sit down, and this bloke starts smiling and chatting away, talking about how our daughter was one of the bright sparks, so hard working...

DAVID   So you knew something was wrong.

RUTH   We were a little taken aback.

YASH   He's going on and on about her natural flair for science. And then he tells us Rachel's scored 80 percent or something in a recent test.

MATT   80 percent?

RACHEL   Don't sound so shocked! You're supposed to be on my side.

MATT   Sorry, just... I remember helping you with your physics homework... 80% seems a bit unlikely.

RUTH   All the teachers had these big books that they would be using to keep track of everyone's marks, and you had that awful habit of trying to read everybody else's score upside down.

YASH   To see how my children compared to the rest of the class, I stand by it. Paid off on this occasion, didn't it? So I'm half listening to what the man is going on about, whilst trying to peer into the book and see the other marks.

RUTH   Not so subtly, might I add.

YASH   I had to, really. I mean, how easy was this test if Rachel could get 80%?

RACHEL   This conversation is doing wonders for my confidence.

YASH   I'm looking down the list, and 80 seems like one of the highest scores, so I'm quite pleased about that. My daughter, is a physics genius. What a thought.

RUTH   And then...

YASH   And then I see Rachel's name. And next to it is her score. And to my complete shock, that score is not 80.

MATT   No!

YASH It's 53. Or somewhere thereabouts.

MATT Well, that's less surprising.

RACHEL Oi.

YASH A million thoughts rush into my head. Has he written it down wrong? Has he read it wrong?

RACHEL Or did he just not know who I am?

YASH I don't know what to think. How do I point this out? Do I just leave it?

RUTH What do you think he does?

DAVID Can't imagine you'd just leave it.

RUTH No, he blurts out –

YASH As I recall, I softly and politely mentioned the mistake.

RUTH You said words to the effect of: "That's not our daughter".

YASH Succinct, precise, to the point.

RUTH Rude.

YASH He was the one being rude. Hadn't even bothered to learn which of his students was which.

RACHEL It was worse than that.

MATT What do you mean?

RACHEL Nothing.

DAVID So what did he do?

YASH He went bright red, apologised for the mistake, then carried on.

RUTH Except he did put on a stern face at that point.

YASH Started using phrases like "needs to pull her socks up".

MATT That is outrageous.

RUTH Well, all in the past.

YASH We don't blame him. Got a good result in the end, didn't you?

RACHEL Yeah, no thanks to him.

MATT Thanks to anyone else?

RACHEL You helped a lot.

MATT I know I did.

RUTH Who knew all these years later that the two of you would finally get together.

DAVID I wouldn't have called it.

RACHEL Me neither.

MATT Really? You don't think there was a bit of a spark back then?

RACHEL Nope. You were just the nerd helping me get good grades.

MATT Charming.

YASH Is this what you meant then, when you said he picked on you?

RUTH What else have we got in here?

RACHEL I don't know... He was just always saying little things, rude names, insults. But just specific people.

RUTH Fewer costumes and dressing up as she got older, you'll see. She seemed to grow into the head shape.

MATT Why do you say it like that? Which "specific people"?

RACHEL Let's leave it. I don't want to say something and then you tell me it's all just in my head.

MATT No one's going to say –

RUTH Oh, did you see this one?

PASSING　　　　　　　　　　　　　　　　　　**89**

RUTH seems oblivious to the conversation, engrossed in the photo book.

RACHEL　　I just... Had this perception, at the time and looking back, that... the students he seemed to favour happened to be the... Caucasian students. And the ones he picked on were...

DAVID　　　The non-Caucasian students?

RACHEL　　Yeah.

YASH　　　 Well. I do believe you've made that up.

RACHEL　　Dad.

YASH　　　 Just a joke.

MATT　　　That's very much not a joke. You seriously think –?

RACHEL　　Don't do that to me. I said I didn't want to say it.

MATT　　　Right, but – I just have no memory of that kind of thing.

RACHEL　　Well you wouldn't, would you?

MATT　　　I'm not saying you're wrong...

RACHEL　　I'm not looking for an argument about it.

RUTH　　　Yes, I most certainly hope not. Now what's this photo of?

MATT　　　Rach, I'm not trying to argue with you.

RACHEL　　Drop it, then.

RUTH　　　What's this big orange blob?

YASH　　　 Perhaps if you gave us an example?

RACHEL　　No, Dad, I don't want to do this.

RUTH　　　Covers half the photo.

MATT　　　You had Davies as a teacher too?

DAVID　　　Let me stop you.

RUTH　　　You know, I think it might be... Yes, I think

it's someone's thumb covering the lens.

MATT Did you notice –?

DAVID I don't wanna get into my whole experience at that place. Then again, Rach, a racist teacher is a pretty big accusation.

RACHEL Whose side are you on? Or do you just oppose everyone and everything?

RUTH Now why on earth would I include a photo like this in the book?

They all look at her for a moment, surprised at her obliviousness.

MATT So are we just going to leave this then?

RACHEL Oh for God's sake. There were just... A lot of things happened to make me believe – Even that story you told...

YASH He was perfectly pleasant to me... no hint of racial bias. Just an idiot.

RACHEL Do you remember the name of the student he got me mixed up with?

YASH Of course I don't.

RACHEL Her name was Shivani Patel.

RUTH Oh, Shivani was a lovely girl. I think there's a picture of her here somewhere.

MATT Hang on –

RACHEL Do you remember Shivani?

MATT Yeah, of course I do.

RACHEL Then perhaps you could tell everyone a little bit about Shivani. For instance, I don't know, her ethnicity?

DAVID I think we get it, Rach.

RACHEL Two girls in the class that happen to not fit

PASSING

into the otherwise all encompassing category of, well, white... And he mixes up the names.

MATT But that's not proof –

RACHEL See, this is why I didn't want to do this.

YASH So he didn't know all the names of the students, or couldn't match names to faces.

RUTH A lot of those teachers were a little questionable. Oh, time to check the oven. Must be nearly there now.

She exits, humming jovially.

RACHEL No matter what kind of evidence I provide, your automatic setting – everyone's setting – is to just... Defend. And you make me feel like I'm crazy...

MATT We're not trying to make you feel that way.

YASH Then again, on the evidence presented...

RACHEL Alright then how about this? "Sing, sing a song".

She sings this to the tune of The Carpenters song "Sing". Pause, they all stare at her.

DAVID What's happening now?

RACHEL You don't remember? Davies used to sing that. All the time, to me.

MATT Oh. I mean I vaguely recall –

RACHEL He used to say my name: "Rachel Singh", and then sing that line. Under his breath or to the whole class. "Singh, Singh a song".

YASH What an absurd thing to do.

MATT Did he do that to you?

DAVID Actually, I think he might have.

RACHEL Not always just that song, but... Mostly.

DAVID Yeah – yes. No I do remember. Not that one

though. "Singh-in' in the Rain". Yeah, that's what it was for me.

YASH You're not serious.

RACHEL No, it's true. There were others...

DAVID "And Your Bird Can Singh"

RACHEL Yep. "Cha-Singh Cars". Remember when that came out? Couldn't get away from it.

DAVID "Ama-Singh Grace".

RACHEL Yeah, that was a bad one.

YASH "Dan-Singh Queen"?

DAVID Don't join in. You weren't there.

MATT I'm sorry, but I don't see how that makes Davies racist.

DAVID Racism is in the eye of the beholder.

RACHEL By deliberately picking on the students with funny sounding names...

DAVID It's a microaggression, at the very least.

YASH A what?

MATT That can't possibly be a conscious thing.

RACHEL I didn't say he was consciously racist. I didn't even say racist.

DAVID Racially prejudiced. I think that's what you implied.

MATT I mean that he can't have deliberately picked on students because of foreign surnames. If you took a sample of everyone he ever taught... I bet he did that with loads of people.

RACHEL Yes, loads of non-Caucasian people...

MATT Non-Caucasian people don't have a monopoly on names that can be made into puns.

RACHEL You just can't see it. You can't even relate to

what I'm talking about.

DAVID   Some people just weren't picked on at school, Rach.

MATT   Alright, I had my fair share –

RACHEL   I'm not talking about a bit of bullying, you know what I'm saying. You had it too.

DAVID   I have to say... Don't jump down my throat, but... Yes, there was a lot of stuff, comments and... You do get treated differently. But, like, is that any different from being singled out for being... I dunno, overweight? Or...

YASH   Or that kid with the bright orange hair.

MATT   Finn something.

RACHEL   That is not in any way the same.

YASH   He was teased quite a lot wasn't he?

RACHEL   This isn't teasing...

DAVID   Rach, don't take this the wrong way, but... I'm just not sure it's as big a deal –

RACHEL   It's not a big deal?

DAVID   Not that it's not a big deal, just that you might be blowing it a bit out of proportion?

RACHEL   What's out of proportion? The fact that you quit playing football, is that out of proportion?

DAVID   That was different.

RACHEL   Was it?

DAVID   I just didn't get on with the guys on the team.

RACHEL   Because they bullied you. For being Indian. Because to a racist, Indian people are good at cricket, not football. That's what you told me. And you just completely ditched something you loved because of a few harmless comments?

DAVID You're twisting it.

RACHEL Am I? Do you remember when we were in sixth form, I cut off all my hair? It was really short.

MATT Yeah, I remember. It looked really good.

RACHEL I wore it like that for ages. Very western style, very Emma Watson. Very in at the time. Do you know why I did that?

DAVID You fancied a change?

RACHEL I did it after weeks of putting up with this group of kids who would sit behind me in Maths, playing this game where they would tear up little bits of paper and see how many they could throw and get stuck in my hair. Because I had hair like no one else. Long, thick, curly black hair.

YASH You never told us this.

RACHEL What could you do? The teacher did nothing. I tried everything to make them stop. But they carried on. So, eventually, I just took away the playing field...

Pause. She walks over to the photo book RUTH has left, and flips through it slowly.

MATT Rach, I really had no idea...

RACHEL Look. Here's the first photo with my new hair. It was really good wasn't it?

YASH That's all very well and good –

DAVID Is it well and good, Dad?

YASH I just don't really know what you're complaining about.

RACHEL I think I might be fighting a losing battle here.

DAVID Please don't do "In my day –"

YASH In my day, kids didn't mask their insults with pop culture wordplay.

DAVID That was a teacher –

YASH If they wanted to make fun of someone, they came right out and said it. They got really in your face about it. In the playground, on the bus. In front of parents and teachers, who wouldn't say anything, of course. And I'm talking about horrible, rude language, none of this Carpenter's nonsense. I can't tell you how many times I was called –

RACHEL Alright, Dad, we get it.

YASH And who was there to put a stop to that?

RACHEL If you think about it for more than a second, somebody obviously did put a stop to it, because, as you say, things aren't as bad as that now.

YASH So then what are you whinging about?

RACHEL I'm not whinging, Dad.

DAVID She's just pointing out that, although things have come a long way since you were a kid, they're still not perfect.

YASH What's not perfect? Explain it to me. All of that stuff, it doesn't stick with you. Look at what I had to go through, and I'm fine. Kids are just soft these days.

DAVID Please shut up.

MATT Maybe there is a bit of a generational disconnect...

YASH Always looking for something to whine about.

RACHEL Oh, fuck off.

They are a little shocked by this.

DAVID Language, Rachel!

YASH Now, I won't have that. We're having a reasonable debate here.

RACHEL You're being utterly obtuse, as always.

YASH There is no need for character assassinations.

MATT As your mum would say, this doesn't need to be an argument, just a discussion.

RACHEL You can fuck off too.

MATT Hey!

YASH Rachel...

RACHEL Stop talking to me like I'm a child.

YASH Then stop behaving –

RACHEL And you. This is a discussion you don't qualify to join.

MATT Don't turn on me –

RACHEL Sorry. Ta-ta. Come back when you've been asked whether you're dropping out of school for an arranged marriage. Or for the umpteenth time someone's asked you why your brother doesn't wear a bloody turban when your surname's Singh, and you have to calmly explain that whilst typically a Sikh name, it's also a pretty common surname for North Indian Hindus.

MATT I get it, Rach, it wasn't the same for me.

RACHEL Or how about when someone's asked you how much your dowry is going to be. Or when someone has the gall to ask you if the new spot that broke out on your forehead overnight is a "Hindu thing"?

DAVID That's hilarious.

MATT Do you mean a bindi?

RACHEL Yes. I do mean a fucking bindi. Have you ever had one of your blackheads likened to a popular cultural accessory?

MATT No.

RACHEL No. Do you know how many times I've been

asked how my dad's Londis business is going?

YASH What? I don't run a newsagents.

RACHEL Or if he drives an uber?

YASH I mostly certainly do not. Why would they ask these things?

DAVID They're stereotypes, Dad.

RACHEL Exactly. Racial stereotypes, which kids are smart enough to know, and to use with malice.

MATT But what about –?

RACHEL Oh, please, please give me an example of a stereotype of white people, how refreshing. Because that's exactly the same. Go on, tell me one damaging stereotype about straight white males that you've suffered through your entire life?

DAVID White men can't jump.

Slight pause. RACHEL smiles at DAVID's joke, though no one else dares to.

RACHEL I'm not just making this up. There is evidence that people of colour suffer, throughout their entire school experience. Passed over in entrance exams, marked down by teachers –

MATT In schools around the country –

RACHEL No, not just –

MATT Not in our school. Like your dad says, things have moved on. Discrimination isn't like it used to be. And we didn't have a bullying problem at school. Don't you remember all those anti-bullying assemblies?

DAVID Oh, come off it.

RACHEL I'm not talking about a bullying problem. I'm talking about a race – Not even a problem, just a...

DAVID A lack of focus.

RACHEL Right... An ignorance of it.

YASH Of race?

RACHEL Yes.

YASH And that's an issue? There were, what? Five ethnic kids in your year at school?

DAVID People of colour, Dad.

RACHEL Right, and that's part of the problem!

YASH I thought it wasn't a problem?

MATT Look, Rach. If I'm allowed to say something... We're not all against you. We're just trying to be rational about this.

RACHEL As am I.

MATT You can't blame us if... Based solely on these examples you've given... We don't agree there was evidence of racial discrimination inherent in the school. Without more data –

RACHEL And why is it that what I know to be true from my experience isn't enough data for you to believe?

Slight pause. The YASH makes a noise of derision.

YASH Kids these days. Making something out of nothing.

Slight pause.

RACHEL You know, maybe none of this would be problematic at all if our differences weren't quite so painstakingly obvious for kids to point out.

YASH What are you blaming me for now? So ungrateful.

RACHEL If we had even one set of family friends that wasn't...

YASH You get what you're dealt, Rachel.

RACHEL I'm just saying. Then things might be a little clearer. We wouldn't feel so... Alone, and in the middle of it all. Can't you see that your decisions have put us in this community... Into this culture, which has made us stand out... So much that we force ourselves to blend in. And we lose...

DAVID What's the alternative? You'd rather if he was setting up an arranged marriage for you?

RACHEL Don't be so flippant all the time.

DAVID That's literally my entire role in this family.

RACHEL There's got to be some middle ground. Otherwise... If one community is going to take every opportunity to point out that we don't fit in with them – and they do, whatever you all think, they do make that clear. And on the other side we're not able to engage with the other community because... Because we weren't raised that way... Then where does that leave us? What do we have that's ours, that you've given us?

YASH You're looking in the wrong place for an explanation. My father settled here. He sent me to my school. I made the friends I made. White friends, I'm not going to apologise for that. And I am grateful for everything –

RACHEL I'm not ungrateful, I'm just asking for some clarity, is that too much? I just want some fucking –

YASH And when you attack me –

DAVID No one's attacking you!

YASH – you attack Grandma and Grandad. You have no respect –

RACHEL I have nothing but respect for Grandad, and I have nothing but contempt for –

RUTH bursts in from the hall. She is carrying two three-tier cake stands – one in each hand. Each one is piled high with an assortment of Indian snack foods: samosas, bhajis, pakoras, aloo tikki, and multiple accompanying chutneys. She also carries a plastic bag with a record in.

RUTH Mountains of food, as requested!

YASH Wow.

MATT Literally mountains.

RUTH It's all just been in the oven, shop bought. As Rachel said, maybe one day we could make it all from scratch.

DAVID All this? You're joking.

RACHEL This all looks amazing, Mum.

RUTH Thank you. Now, before we dig in to all of this, I've got a little surprise for you, Rachel. Well, for all of you really.

YASH Can this wait until we've eaten?

RUTH No, it can't. If I don't do it now... I think I never will! Oh my stomach's absolutely full of butterflies.

YASH My stomach is absolutely empty...

RUTH No touching the food until I say so.

RACHEL What's going on, Mum?

RUTH Patience, patience. Now...

She hands YASH the bag.

RUTH Please will you put this record on? And everyone get comfortable, please! Alright, here we go.

She exits quickly. RACHEL, DAVID and MATT settle on the sofa, uneasy, caught of guard by this change of pace. YASH obediently puts the record on; it is "Mehndi Laga Ke Rakhna" from Dilwale Dulhania Le Jayenge. Choreographed with the music, RUTH enters again. Obviously nervous, she makes her way to the centre of the room and dances along to the music. The moves she uses are in the classic Bollywood style, and though she makes many mistakes in the timing and execution, she gets more and more into the dance as the song progresses. Throughout, she is egged on by MATT, YASH and DAVID, who applaud, cheer, and encourage. RACHEL stares in disbelief. Suddenly, she runs to the record player and turns it off – perhaps with such force that the needle scratches along the record.

YASH   Rachel!

DAVID   What are you doing?

RUTH   What's going on?

RACHEL   What's going –? You're asking me what's going on? What the hell do you think you're doing?

RUTH   What do you –? Is something the matter?

RACHEL   You can't honestly think what you're doing is ok. Surely.

RUTH   Everyone seemed to be having a good time...

RACHEL   It's disgustingly offensive.

Pause.

RUTH   I see.

DAVID   Don't listen to Rachel, Mum. We were enjoying it.

RUTH   No, no. That's alright. I shouldn't...

RACHEL   Mum – Shit. Look, I didn't mean...

RUTH   I didn't know. I didn't know it was wrong to...

DAVID   It's not wrong, Mum.

RACHEL   I only meant –

RUTH   I did it for you. For today. I just wanted... Everything to be special for you today. Excuse me.

She exits quickly, failing to conceal tears. Pause.

DAVID   Why did you do that?

RACHEL   I'm sorry, but –

YASH   No. No buts. How dare you. How dare you speak to your mother that way?

RACHEL   Dad, she can't do stuff like that... It's hugely inappropriate.

YASH   The only thing that's been hugely inappropriate today is the way you have acted.

RACHEL   Oh, right, but when –

YASH   Stop it. Be quiet, for once. And think.

RACHEL   I'm not wrong...

YASH   You know. I don't have a lot of advice to impart, I really don't. I haven't grown wise as the years have gone by. But I learnt one thing a long time ago that you might find useful to think about. Logic, rationality and social morality... They mean nothing when you're dealing with loved ones. You need your own set of rules for family.

He exits to the hall.

RACHEL   You've got to know that wasn't right.

DAVID   Save it.

RACHEL   I wasn't trying to –

DAVID   Then what the fuck were you trying to do?

He exits to the hall. RACHEL looks after him, then turns her gaze to MATT. He says nothing, just looks at her sadly. After a while, MATT takes a samosa from one of the plates and nibbles at the corner without enthusiasm. Lights fade slowly.

ACT II, SCENE 2

Lights up. The room is as it was at the end of the previous act. YASH and RUTH are standing together near the door, speaking in hushed tones.

RUTH No. Absolutely not.

YASH I'm fine to go.

RUTH You've had far too much.

YASH It's been spread out over the day, it's moved through my system. Ruth...

RUTH No. Don't say it. I'm fine.

YASH Are you?

RUTH Yes. I think so. Yash... I'm really trying...

YASH I know you are! Of course you are.

RUTH I'm trying to be supportive.

YASH No one's trying harder than you. You're wonderful. It's more than she deserves.

RUTH She resents me...

YASH She doesn't. Stop it now.

Her voice breaks for a moment, and she speaks more loudly than she means to.

RUTH What else can I do? What more can I...

Slight pause, he comforts her.

YASH It'll all be ok after today. You know families. Temperatures run high. Particularly this family.

RUTH She's saying a lot...

YASH You have to take everything with a pinch –

RUTH Not everything. She's right about some things.

YASH We shouldn't let her insult us –

RUTH We can listen. We can think about...

Another pause.

YASH I thought it was wonderful.

RUTH It's fine, you don't have to –

YASH Really very sexy...

RUTH Oh, hush. Stop it! Stop it now.

MATT enters from the hall, and stops when he sees them.

MATT Sorry... I didn't realise anyone was in here. I just came to get... Well, truthfully, I came for another samosa, they're absolutely delicious.

RUTH I'm glad someone liked them.

MATT I can't get enough of them. And this sauce, what is it?

RUTH It's a date and tamarind chutney.

MATT Amazing.

YASH Homemade, you know.

MATT No!

RUTH Just blended a few things together. I'm happy to hear it's a winner.

DAVID enters from the hall.

DAVID Save a couple for me. You alright, Mum?

RUTH Yes. No, yes. Fine, fine. Now, I really need to get going.

DAVID Where are you –?

YASH Nowhere. As I've said, I'm more than happy to go.

RUTH And I've said no.

DAVID Are you going to get Grandad? Can I come?

RUTH No, you stay here. I'll be back very soon. But... Just be aware, if he's not up to coming...

Slight pause, understanding between them.

DAVID If you are going, whatever you do, don't forget to pick up some matches or a lighter.

RUTH Heavens, yes. Better not. Alright. Back soon.

She exits to the foyer.

YASH I know what you're going to ask.

DAVID Alright. What's the answer then?

YASH Your mother insisted on going herself.

DAVID Is someone a little over the limit?

YASH Don't be ridiculous.

DAVID It's not exactly ludicrous to accuse you –

YASH When I'm drunk, you'll know about it.

He exits quickly to the hall.

DAVID Yes, I expect I will.

He ponders for a second or two, then seems to notice MATT again.

DAVID Still here? Haven't had enough yet?

MATT This is nothing. You should see my family play charades. Gets quite violent. Sure everything's ok?

DAVID Yeah. It's not you. I mean, obviously it's not you. You're just here.

MATT Thanks...

DAVID I'm sorry you have to take all this on.

MATT It's really nothing...

DAVID It's not nothing.

MATT No. It's not.

DAVID At least you know I'm not the crazy one, right?

MATT I wouldn't say anyone is crazy...

DAVID Really? No offence or anything, but Rachel's completely off the rails today. Even more than usual.

MATT None taken.
DAVID What?
MATT I won't take offence.
DAVID Right.
MATT She's going through something right now.
DAVID Aren't we all.
MATT Yes. Looks that way.
DAVID You mean with me and him?

He indicates towards the kitchen.

DAVID It's always like this. We disagree, that's what fathers and sons do.
MATT I don't think you're really disagreeing about anything.
DAVID What family have you been watching all day?

RACHEL enters, not so sure of herself when she sees DAVID. She is now wearing an oversized men's hoodie and jeans.

RACHEL Hi.
MATT Hey, you changed?
RACHEL Had another shower. Where's mum?
DAVID If you're looking to apologise you're too late.
MATT She went to pick up your grandad.
RACHEL Why didn't Dad –?
DAVID Why do you think?
RACHEL Typical.

Pause. Eventually DAVID can't stand the silence.

DAVID "Dan-Singh Queen", that was a good one, wasn't it? Wonder why Davies never thought of that one.
MATT He was an idiot, remember?

RACHEL Thought you liked him?

MATT I have a no tolerance policy for racists.

RACHEL I don't really think he was racist. I never said that. I never meant that...

MATT We get it.

RACHEL Just subconsciously I think...

DAVID Right, microaggressions...

RACHEL Yeah...

MATT We know what you meant.

DAVID Maybe it's better to steer away from the subject of school altogether.

RACHEL But why? Why do I... Whenever I look back at memories I thought were... why do I look at them with this sense of unease? Like my childhood and teenage years were anything other than absolutely fine.

DAVID Now you know more... You can see that stuff was there.

RACHEL You can see it too?

DAVID It's not something I want to go looking for.

RACHEL Neither do I! That's the last thing I want to do. Please don't get me wrong... I'm not looking for things to complain about. I'm not saying that anything that happened has negatively affected my life in any way...

MATT Then... And please don't take this the wrong way, but... Why does any of it matter?

DAVID Because it was there. You're right... It did happen.

RACHEL We have to acknowledge that it wasn't right. I haven't convinced you.

MATT   I'd like to talk about it more.

DAVID   That's a no.

RACHEL   I'm not sure there's much more to say.

Pause. The silence hangs between MATT and RACHEL, and again DAVID is desperate to break it.

DAVID   You know, I was thinking about this whole bullying thing. I think maybe they didn't really know what to look for sometimes, or how to stamp it out. But, you know that kid Finn? Finn Byrne was his name. I'm still friends with him on Facebook – he works for an insurance company now. He was probably the most picked on kid I can remember, and he is absolutely fine in adult life. As soon as you get out of school, it doesn't matter that you have ginger hair, it's not going to hold you back in life. Or if you're chubby, or tall – anything kids would make fun of. And I really, really hate to say this, but... There's something about not being white that doesn't get left behind with the rest of the playground bullying. I'm gonna...

DAVID gestures toward the door, and exits. Pause.

MATT   Hi.

RACHEL   Hey.

MATT   Just us again.

RACHEL   How's your day going?

MATT   Pretty eventful so far.

RACHEL   Tell me about it. I'm sorry.

MATT   Everyone keeps trying to apologise to me, it's really fine.

RACHEL   It's not weird?

MATT   I'm not saying it's not been a strange day...

RACHEL   I am sorry. When we all get together I act so –

MATT   Different.

RACHEL   Do you think so?
MATT   Different to when we're alone, yeah.
RACHEL   I can keep saying sorry...
MATT   You don't have to.
Pause.
MATT   Why didn't you tell me any of that stuff?
RACHEL   Are you angry with me?
MATT   Don't you think I deserved to know?
RACHEL   You know now.
MATT   Do you not... feel comfortable with me?
RACHEL   How can I just bring this up? When I know how you're going to act.
MATT   What do you mean?
RACHEL   I'm not blaming you. Really, I get it. It's hard to challenge things, even for me. So for you...
MATT   No, it's not that hard. There was something wrong at school, ok, I can get on board with that. But you said yourself, it hasn't affected your life-
RACHEL   But it has. Not consciously, I can't... But it's there. It's shaped me. It's made me who I am.
MATT   How?
RACHEL   Can we please just...?
MATT   No, we always say let's just talk about it later. We can't just keep kicking the can down the road, let's talk.
RACHEL   I can't right now, Matt.
MATT   No that's not fair, Rach. I'm sorry but... I've been here, I've done my best and I'm trying to give you the support you need but you have to let me in!
RACHEL   If I say this... It'll change things.
MATT   It won't change the way I feel. Please, Rach.

Slight pause.

RACHEL Look at me. Do you see an Indian person? Do you see me the same way you see the women in Aamir Khan films I've made you watch? Or do you see a British girl that you went to school with? The same as all the others. She just happens to be a different shade, but she's the same on the inside.

MATT I see you.

RACHEL What does that *mean*? You've been told your whole life not to see people of colour any differently to you. Because everyone's the same. And they are. But in a community where 90% of the people you meet are white, and the other 10% who aren't white are treated by the nice middle class white liberal folks as if they are the same... What does that make them? Are they just... White too?

MATT Of course not!

RACHEL And if they don't celebrate Diwali... And they don't like sitar music, and they don't wear a sari or a fucking bindi, and they don't even really like tadka dal... What does that make them? In what way are they not different to you? In what way are they not white?

Pause.

RACHEL I'm sorry.
MATT No, don't be.
RACHEL Is that what you wanted?
MATT In a way, yeah.
RACHEL Good. That's good.
MATT I'm not sure it's good...
RACHEL No, but...
MATT I'm glad you told me. But...
RACHEL What?

MATT   Do you blame me?

RACHEL   Nothing is an attack on you.

MATT   Right, but as one of those middle class white liberal folk you were talking about... Do you, I don't know, do you resent me?

Pause.

RACHEL   I'm not sure how to answer that.

Pause.

MATT   I see.

RACHEL   No. I don't mean- No, I don't resent you. How could it be your fault?

MATT   Something makes you hesitant.

RACHEL   I need to unpack everything.

MATT   We need to unpack everything...

RACHEL   No. I need to.

MATT   I can help.

RACHEL   Can you?

MATT   Of course, it'll be easier together... I was wrong, I shouldn't have said- I was being defensive. I'm sorry.

RACHEL   It's not even about school, Matt...

MATT   Then what is it?

RACHEL   Look... I just can't do it. I can't...

MATT   Can't what? Please talk to me, I want to understand!

RACHEL   How can I make you understand something that I don't even understand myself?

MATT   We'll work it out.

RACHEL   How will we? With you making me second guess myself, asking me if it really matters? That's what you said.

MATT   I'm just trying to wrap my head around it all.

RACHEL And you calling me crazy. 'You know how she can be'.

MATT I said I didn't mean anything by that.

RACHEL So what's the solution? You expect me to pull up painful stuff to the surface just to... To educate you? To desperately try to change your mind? I don't even care that you disagree about Davies or school or... Don't try to argue, I know that you think differently. But that's the problem, Matt, we're different, and fundamentally you just can't get it...

Pause.

MATT I don't know what I'm supposed to say.

RACHEL Maybe, this time, there isn't something you can say to fix it just like that. I need time. To do this by myself. I don't know where my place is, Matt, and being with you... I've loved being together but it's... One too many layers of confusion.

MATT What does that mean?

Pause. They both know where this is heading.

MATT I can give you time. And space. Yeah. Maybe we should leave this now and – and, think for a little while. And then we can see how we feel. How you feel.

RACHEL I'm telling you how I feel.

MATT I know, I know you are. Just...

RACHEL Just what?

MATT Just, sometimes... In the moment you can say things, and later you feel...

RACHEL Not this time.

MATT I'm just saying maybe we could take some time, cool off, and then –

RACHEL I'm not angry, I don't need to calm down-

MATT I didn't say calm down –

RACHEL I'm not being irrational. You always... Listen to what I'm saying, this is how I feel.

MATT This isn't how it's supposed to go. Rach, please. There's a pattern... I say the wrong thing, I do the wrong – And you're not happy with me but then we make it right...

RACHEL Doesn't sound like a very healthy cycle, does it?

MATT You're confused and you're worried, and I said the wrong thing–

RACHEL It's not about that. I don't want to force us back to a good place anymore.

MATT Rach, please don't throw this away.

RACHEL Don't –

MATT I love –

RACHEL Stop.

Pause. MATT is struggling to contain his emotions, trying to force himself to remain calm.

MATT Suddenly I don't think it's a good idea for me to be here. I should probably...

RACHEL Yeah.

Pause. She's expecting him to move but he can't bring himself to go.

MATT This is insane... Your dad's talking about us moving in together and here we are... Are you... Are you sure this is what...

She nods.

RACHEL I'm really glad you... were here.

Slight pause. Matt nods slightly and tries to pull himself together to leave.

MATT Please thank your parents for having me.

RACHEL   What do I say?

MATT   I don't – Just tell them I had my own Diwali celebration to get to.

He can't find the right words, or any. He goes to exit.

RACHEL   Matt, wait.

She approaches him to give him one last hug.

MATT   Don't. Just... Bye, Rach. Happy Diwali.

He exits to the foyer. Left alone, RACHEL's whole body seems to exhale. Perhaps for the first time we see her without the nervous energy that has compelled her thus far. DAVID enters quietly.

DAVID   Where's Matt?

RACHEL   He had to step out.

DAVID   Is he coming back?

RACHEL looks at him.

DAVID   I'm... Um, sorry to hear that.

RACHEL   Thanks. This is all pointless, isn't it?

DAVID   Don't ask me. I don't know what you thought today would achieve. I mean did you want us all up dancing around singing Hari Krishna, or would you say that was offensive too?

RACHEL   God, David, don't be so – You just don't get it.

DAVID   You're right there. I don't understand anything. Everything you're asking for is contradictory.

RACHEL   You *really* don't get it.

DAVID   No, I really don't. Explain this to me. You're complaining about not having access to all these things that you suddenly want. Right? Let's take mum and dad out of the equation for a second, however much you want to blame them. You want more Indian things in your life, to be seen as, whatever. But then you rage about the fact that kids and teachers noticed us for the differences between us and the rest of them. How can you expect people to treat you differently and the same simultaneously?

RACHEL That's not what I'm doing.

DAVID You can't normalise something and expect to be unique at the same time.

RACHEL You know what I don't understand? Why you don't feel exactly the same as I do.

DAVID It's just not an issue for me. I'm happy to be...

RACHEL What? To be what?

DAVID I'm happy with how our lives have been.

RACHEL For god's sake. I'm not saying that I'm unhappy –

DAVID What are you saying then, Rach?

RACHEL Just that... I wish things were different. Certain things.

DAVID Why though?

RACHEL I don't know. For the sake of clarity.

DAVID That can't be –

RACHEL Because I'm scared.

DAVID Scared of what?

RACHEL Everything.

DAVID What does that mean?

RACHEL So much...

DAVID Rach, you have to talk to me.

RACHEL What good will it do?

DAVID What harm will it do?

Slight pause.

RACHEL I'm scared. I'm scared that these things which are supposed to be a part of me, aren't there in my personality. I'm scared that I'm missing out on things, losing things, that were supposed to be passed down to me through our family. But they got thrown out somewhere to make way for British shit. The language, the dress, the customs and spirituality and, yeah, the festivals. I'm scared of losing them forever when Grandad... Because try as I might to think otherwise, I have to face the reality that it's not going to be long. And I'm scared that it's already too late...

DAVID Rach, you don't have to-

RACHEL And you know what else? I'm scared that, for the most part, I have totally assimilated into a... White culture, whatever that is. Because of the lack of people who look like me, who can share in what little culture I have received... I'm scared that the way I act, the way I speak, the way I dress... All that makes me just...

DAVID White?

RACHEL And... Most of all... I'm scared that no one can tell the difference. That my skin... That I can just pass for...

DAVID You don't look-

RACHEL And I'll just lose it all, and no one will ever know it was ever there in the first place.

DAVID Rach, I...

RACHEL You want to know the worst thing? Because of the way I look, my class, my mother's skin colour... I'm scared that I fall into some open fucking middle void, and that I really don't have the right to be scared about anything.

DAVID You have the right.

RACHEL I want more than that... I want a place on

the scale. I want to know what I am. I don't want to just pass for something... I want to be.

Pause.

RACHEL I just wanted everything to go right today. So we could pretend... So it would feel like all our heritage isn't so fucking... Alien to us.

DAVID I get it.

RACHEL Do you?

DAVID I mean, I think so.

Slight pause.

RACHEL You don't have to say anything else.

DAVID How do you know I was going to?

RACHEL You've got your thinking face on.

DAVID Didn't realise I had a thinking face.

RACHEL It's just nice to say it all out loud. I don't need you to agree. And I definitely don't need you to argue.

DAVID Alright.

Another pause.

DAVID Let me say one thing.

RACHEL Spit it out.

DAVID Look, I do get it. At least, I think... I see where you're coming from.

RACHEL But?

DAVID But... Don't blame Mum, ok? It's not her fault–

RACHEL This again? I'm not saying I blame-

DAVID Let me finish. It's not her fault she's white. I know you think that's the root of the problem... Don't resent her for it when all she does is to try to help you.

RACHEL It just comes out.

DAVID We all say things we don't mean. Look who you're talking to.

Slight pause.

DAVID What you said about Grandad...

RACHEL I just meant... He really is getting better every day. But...

DAVID But you're still scared?

RACHEL Yeah. I am.

DAVID Me too.

Slight pause, then suddenly YASH bursts through the door from the hall. He advances to his record player and starts flipping through his collection.

RACHEL Dad? Everything ok?

Pause. YASH doesn't answer, he just looks through his collection. RACHEL looks to DAVID for an answer, but he just shrugs. YASH finds the record he was looking for, pulls it out and turning to RACHEL and DAVID. It is the self titled album "Velvet Underground & Nico".

YASH Velvet Underground.

Slight pause.

DAVID What about them?

YASH The album, it's Velvet Underground.

RACHEL And Nico, yes...

YASH puts the record down and turns back to his collection, this time pulling out "Dark Side of the Moon" by Pink Floyd.

YASH Not just that. This too.

RACHEL Ok...

YASH Too obvious?

DAVID What are you–?

YASH No, you're right. Here, then.

He has now pulled out "John Barleycorn Must Die" by Traffic.

DAVID   What point are you making?

YASH   John Barleycorn, Dark Side of the Moon, Velvet Underground...

RACHEL   And Nico.

YASH   And so much more, don't you see?

RACHEL   Dad...

YASH   Sergeant Pepper. Let it Bleed. Cosmo's Factory. Automatic for the People. Led Zeppelin IV. And Led Zeppelin III, for that matter. Elvis Presley – the album, not the artist. But the artist too. Elvis bloody Presley. Freddie Mercury. And George Harrison. Bob Dylan – that song of his that makes you cry. Simple Twist of Fate. Sam Cooke singing Bring it on Home. Simon and Garfunkel's harmonies on Sound of Silence. The guitar hook in Sultans of Swing. The piano riff in the middle of Scenes from an Italian Restaurant. Blue bloody Monday.

Pause. He is out of breath. The others stare at him.

YASH   I didn't give you everything. I didn't give you what you wanted, evidently. And I'm... Sorry, for that. I'm sorry I didn't give you your heritage. But I gave you parts of myself, I gave you... I gave you what I loved.

RACHEL   I know, Dad.

YASH   I guess that's the best I could give you.

RACHEL   And that's enough. You don't have to be sorry. I'm grateful for all of it. Everything you gave me.

Slight pause, the two smile at each other.

RACHEL   Except Led Zeppelin III. You can have that back.

DAVID   I was going to say...

YASH Oh, come off it, you haven't listened to Led Zeppelin III.

DAVID I've heard Immigrant Song, that was enough for me.

YASH It's so much more than that one track.

RACHEL Name one other song on that album.

YASH That one called...

DAVID Yes?

RACHEL What's it called?

YASH Oh, you know. That one with...

DAVID With the guitar? Is that what you were going to say?

YASH Maybe.

Pause again, YASH still has something to say.

YASH I'm not stupid, I know Grandad's not going to live forever. But it's not his time. I haven't... Said everything... That I need to.

Pause. DAVID and RACHEL exchange looks.

DAVID It's not too late, Dad.

YASH I know, son. We have time ahead to get everything right. Even if right now it's...

Slight pause, no one knows what to say next.

DAVID You make that whole speech... I can't believe you forget to mention "Non-Stop Erotic Cabaret". Where would you be without that album in your life?

RACHEL Can you ever take anything seriously?

DAVID I try not to.

They smile. The sound of a car pulling into the driveway outside is heard.

RACHEL Is that –

DAVID Finally.

YASH David, help me get him out of the car, will you?

DAVID Yeah, of course. You coming?

RACHEL You go, I haven't got everything ready.

DAVID and YASH exit to the foyer. RACHEL rushes around retrieving things in a very routine manner, as if she has done this before many times. She clears a specific spot on the sofa and places a few pillows there which she plumps up. She places a few items nearby: a newspaper and a pen on top, some comfy slippers, a folded blanket on the back of the sofa, etc. RUTH enters during this.

RACHEL Mum –

RUTH Hello dear. What have I missed? You didn't try to play another game did you? Come outside, Grandad's –

RACHEL Wait. Mum, I just wanted to say... Thank you. For everything. And I'm really sorry...

RUTH Hush now. All in the past.

RACHEL But... I really am.

RACHEL hugs RUTH.

RUTH I know, darling. Of course I know. Now. Where's Matt gotten to?

RACHEL He had to...

RUTH Oh, Rachel.

RACHEL I'm fine. It's ok, really.

RUTH Will he be back?

RACHEL I...

RUTH Whatever it is, I'm sure the two of you will figure it out.

RACHEL I don't think we will this time.

RUTH Not everyone can handle being part of this

family. Maybe he's just not cut out for it.

RACHEL Yeah, maybe.

RUTH Are you sure –?

RACHEL It's for the best. I think.

RUTH gives RACHEL another hug.

RACHEL Are they coming back in?

RUTH Actually, Grandad's got a little surprise for everyone. But before I forget

RUTH pulls a box of matches out of the carrier bag, holding them out to RACHEL, who takes them.

RACHEL Thank you so so much, mum.

RUTH No need to thank me. Grandad had them all ready, he knew we'd need them, for these.

She reaches into the bag again and pulls out a packet of sparklers.

RACHEL Sparklers!

RUTH He's been talking my ear off in the car about how it's not Diwali without fireworks, so these are in lieu. Another thing to add to the list for next year! He's been stockpiling for ages apparently, since you told him you were doing all of this.

RACHEL I can't believe it. Look at him, I can't remember the last time I saw him this animated.

RUTH He's very excited.

They stand watching out of the window for a moment.

RUTH Better get a move on, if I need to get dinner on as well.

RACHEL Will the snacks reheat ok?

RUTH Another surprise for you. Grandma's famous kidney bean curry. As best as I remember from watching her cook. You'll have to help me rolling out the dough for the puris mind.

RACHEL Mum. You're amazing.

RUTH I wanted it to be perfect for you.

RACHEL I'm...

RACHEL looks like she might cry.

RUTH I know dear.

RACHEL I'm just-

RUTH It's ok. It's going to be ok.

RACHEL Yeah.

RUTH Come on, let's not leave them out there waiting for these.

RACHEL Ok, I'll be out in just one sec.

RUTH smiles reassuringly at her, then exits. RACHEL is left alone on stage, holding the box of matches. She smiles, then picks up one of the diyas on a nearby shelf. She places it on the coffee table, breathing in and out to calm herself, before lighting a match and lighting the diya with it. She takes a moment to admire it, then heads for the door, pausing as she's about to exit. She flicks a switch, and the fairy lights all over the walls come on. Again she admires them for a second before stepping out of the door and pulling it closed behind her.

Lights down.

The End.

Aurora Metro Books

ADA by Emily Holyoake
ISBN 978-1-912430-09-3   £9.99

THREE WOMEN by Matilda Velevitch
ISBN 978-1-912430-35-2   £9.99

COMBUSTION by Asif Khan
ISBN 978-1-911501-91-6   £9.99

DIARY OF A HOUNSLOW GIRL by Ambreen Razia
ISBN 978-0-9536757-9-1   £8.99

SPLIT/MIXED by Ery Nzaramba
ISBN 978-1-911501-97-8   £10.99

A GIRL WITH A BOOK by Nick Wood
ISBN 978-1-910798-61-4   £12.99

THE TROUBLE WITH ASIAN MEN by Sudha Bhuchar, Kristine Landon-Smith and Louise Wallinger
ISBN 978-1-906582-41-8   £8.99

WOMEN OF ASIA by Asa Palomera
ISBN 978-1-906582-94-4   £7.99

HARVEST by Manjula Padmanabhan
ISBN 978-0-9536757-7-7   £6.99

I HAVE BEFORE ME A REMARKABLE DOCUMENT by Sonja Linden
ISBN 978-0-9546912-3-3   £7.99

NEW SOUTH AFRICAN PLAYS ed. Charles J. Fourie
ISBN 978-0-9542330-1-3   £11.99

BLACK AND ASIAN PLAYS Anthology introduced by Afia Nkrumah
ISBN 978-0-9536757-4-6   £12.99

SOUTHEAST ASIAN PLAYS ed. Cheryl Robson and Aubrey Mellor
ISBN 978-1-906582-86-9   £16.99

SIX PLAYS BY BLACK AND ASIAN WOMEN WRITERS ed. Kadija George
ISBN 978-0-9515877-2-0   £12.99

www.aurorametro.com